The Robert Heinlein Interview

Pulpless.Com™ Books by J. Neil Schulman

Novels
  Alongside Night (trade edition forthcoming)
  The Rainbow Cadenza (trade edition forthcoming)

Nonfiction
  The Robert Heinlein Interview and Other Heinleiniana
  Stopping Power: Why 70 Million Americans Own Guns
    (trade edition forthcoming)
  The Frame of the Century? (trade edition forthcoming)
  Book Publishing in the 21st Century, Volumes One and Two

Short Stories
  Nasty, Brutish, and Short Stories (trade edition forthcoming)

Omnibus Collection
  Self Control Not Gun Control

Collected Screenwritings
  Profile in Silver and Other Screenwritings
    (trade edition forthcoming)

J. NEIL SCHULMAN

The
Robert Heinlein
Interview

And Other Heinleiniana

PULPLESS.COM, INC.

775 East Blithedale Ave., Suite 508
Mill Valley, CA 94941, USA.
Voice & Fax: (500) 367-7353
Home Page: http://www.pulpless.com/
Business inquiries to info@pulpless.com
Editorial inquiries & submissions to
editors@pulpless.com

This book was published in slightly different earlier digital editions by SoftServ Publishing Services, Inc., in September 1990; and by Pulpless.Com™ in June, 1996.
First Pulpless.Com™, Inc. Trade Edition May, 1999.

Library of Congress Catalog Card Number: 98-83271

ISBN: 1-58445-015-0

Book and Cover designed by CaliPer, Inc.

Cover Photograph by Julius Schulman © 1999 by Julius Schulman

To Soleil

I'd Like You To Meet An Old Friend Of Mine

Table of Contents

Our Dutch Uncle

Foreword by Brad Linaweaver

"He is in our heads." So writes J. Neil Schulman about his hero, Robert A. Heinlein. My friend of thirty years, Bill Ritch, has used the same phrase as long as I've known him. But just who is the "our?" Do Neil and Bill mean the community of science fiction professionals? Do they mean the fans? I think not.

The "our" refers to an area where two special interests meet: science fiction and libertarianism. For science fiction enthusiasts who are not libertarians (the majority), Heinlein is an important figure in the field and an influence on many writers. For libertarians who are not science fiction readers (the majority), Heinlein is an interesting footnote in the literature of liberty.

But for those of us who combine these two passions and have optimism in the future, Robert Anson Heinlein is God.

We have needed this book for a very long time. As Mrs. Heinlein says in her endorsement, this interview will appeal both to readers of science fiction and to libertarians. But for those of us who burn for technological marvels and want freedom to enjoy them instead of being slaves to a technocratic Big Brother, Heinlein created the blueprint that may get us to a better world. Not Utopia, because he taught us that such a dream truly is nowhere. A better world, on the other hand, is not impossible. It is simply hard to achieve.

When he died, the larger world paid attention to his impact on us; yes, on those of us who take *The Moon is a Harsh Mistress* seriously! As I wrote in *New Libertarian*, the Associated Press mentioned his libertarianism. The science fiction press did its best to ignore the same thing. I was annoyed at the time. Now I see that the SF world was trying to do him a favor by ignoring his politics. They gave him a vacation from their usual slanders and libels.

Now with the Hollywood blockbuster of *Starship Troopers*, the SF community is back to normal; back to calling Heinlein a fascist. And what of his defenders? They know full well that the limited government model of liberty is every bit as objectionable to today's totalitarians as is any anarchy. Those who call Heinlein a fascist know that they are lying. Those who deny Heinlein's libertarianism from the other direction know they are lying, too.

In this, the best interview with Heinlein, Neil Schulman inspired the following comment from his hero: "I would say that my position is not too far from that of Ayn Rand; that I would like to see government reduced to no more than internal police and courts, external armed forces — with the other matters handled otherwise. I'm sick of the way the government sticks its nose into everything, now." Also: "The justification for free enterprise is that it's free."

There is only one kind of mentality in this sorry world that describes such expressions of American individualism as fascist: the Marxist mind. That this discredited mode of thought dominates science fiction criticism is no surprise. It still holds sway in New York and Hollywood. It may be finished in Moscow but it's doing fine at Harvard and Yale.

That is why we need this book. Robert A. Heinlein is our Dutch Uncle. Maybe the American family is falling apart for lack of decent father figures but at least we still have the voice of one sane man who tells us to be the best we can be and expects even more than an Army recruitment ad. (Besides, he's Navy!)

The United States of America beat its greatest enemies of the century. Heinlein was there in the fight against fascism (and its virulent mutant form of Nazism) as well as in the 75-year-long struggle against Soviet Communism. We defeated these monsters and now our reward seems to be domestic tyranny at the hands of our worst elements, true parasites of the soul. Naturally such people cannot stand the work of Robert A. Heinlein. Naturally they accuse the man of propagating what is actually their own evils.

The trouble for them is that Heinlein won't go away. They can't let him go away. The kind of totalitarian who gravitates to the arts needs to steal from somewhere—even from our Dutch Uncle, who was a superb entertainer. But they make sure to leave out his philosophy.

Buy multiple copies! Tell your friends! The web is

here. Trade paperbacks are here. This one book will answer for all time what Heinlein's positions really were.

The answers are not good for the enemies of freedom.

December 27, 1998

Introduction

"What really knocks me out is a book that, when you're all done reading it, you wish the author that wrote it was a terrific friend of yours and you could call him up on the phone whenever you felt like it. That doesn't happen much, though."
—Holden Caulfield in J.D. Salinger's *The Catcher in the Rye*

In July of 1973, I was twenty and had been an avid fan of Robert Heinlein for half my life. I don't think it's an overstatement to say there's a good chance that if he hadn't lived, I would've never made it to age twenty. Teenage suicide is common, and my teenage years were, to state it mildly, not good. If Robert Heinlein hadn't written the books he wrote, and I hadn't read them, I doubt very much that I would have had the intellectual background necessary to climb out of the hole I was in between the ages of fifteen and eighteen.

For most of my childhood, Heinlein represented everything in my life that meant anything to me. He wrote about futures that were worth living for. He wrote about talented people who felt life was worth living, and made it worth living, no matter what the breaks that fell their way. His characters never had an easy time of it, but they persevered.

And, boy oh boy, when you're getting the shit kicked out of you in half a dozen different ways, images like that are sometimes the only thing between you and the edge.

So in July of 1973, only a few short years since I figured he'd saved my life, I'd been looking for a way to phone up Robert Heinlein for quite a while, already. And that was the month I managed to do it, by parlaying a review of one of his novels for one major New York newspaper into an interview with him for another.

I'm not going to repeat that story here; you'll find it later in this book.

When I met Robert Heinlein in person in 1973, a few months after I interviewed him by telephone, he was at the height of his powers as one of the major writers of this century, and I was a writer just starting out. He was sixty-six, and had been writing for thirty-four years. His thirty-eighth book had just been published; his sales figures were higher than ever before. And if your idols are supposed to have clay feet, he kept his well-shod: I was unable to find them.

Heinlein treated me as an equal, even though I didn't feel like an equal. I'll never forget the reception Heinlein held at his New York hotel suite in 1973 in which he introduced me to his East Coast friends, including such luminaries as Herman Kahn, of whom I hadn't even heard at the time I interviewed Heinlein. And it was at this reception that Robert A. Heinlein ended any doubts about his ideology, introducing me to one friend with the words, "Neil and I are libertarians."

For the remainder of his life, Robert Heinlein and I were friends. I sent him birthday presents; he sent a wedding present. We kept up with each other. My excess desire to have him endorse my first novel caused a major problem with my writing career; my misstep, however, did not break up our friendship.

Don't get me wrong. There are lots of people who knew Heinlein far better than I did, and were far better friends with him for far longer. We saw each other in person maybe a half dozen times total, with another dozen or so phone calls scattered between 1973 and his death in 1988. Mostly I wrote him and his wife, Virginia Heinlein; mostly Ginny wrote back. But the important thing in all this is that during the course of our friendship, I was able to tell him how much his writing meant to me.

It was enough.

This book contains articles, reviews, and letters I wrote on Heinlein and his fiction between 1972 and 1988, and two newer pieces, a review of *The Moon Is A Harsh Mistress* written in 1996, and my 1997 remarks upon accepting the Prometheus Hall of Fame Award for *Methuselah's Children*. Each of these have been included because they express one aspect or another of my *gestalt* of Heinlein.

The most important item in this collection, obviously, is the Heinlein interview itself. It is, to the best of Virginia Heinlein's and my knowledge, the longest interview Heinlein ever authorized, and the only interview in which he talked freely and extensively about his personal philosophy and ideological views.

It's going to be obvious, reading this interview, that the interviewer was a young ideologue with an agenda of his own, who wasn't quite sure which he wanted to do more—interview Heinlein or argue politics with him. All to the better: that young squirt got answers out of Heinlein that no one else did. And this older squirt is happy to make it available again.

For those who want to know where Heinlein stood, in his own words, on epistemology, UFO's, life after death, or libertarianism, this interview is a priceless gem. I still can't believe I was lucky enough to get it.

No, strike that. Heinlein, through Dr. Samuel Russell in *Have Space Suit—Will Travel*, said, "There is no such thing as luck. There is only adequate or inadequate preparation to cope with a statistical universe."

And Heinlein, himself, prepared me.

J. Neil Schulman

January, 1999

The Lost Manuals

1988

Sooner or later we all imagine there's a set of technical manuals our parents were supposed to give us at birth with instructions on How Life Works.

Not that thick book called *The Purpose of Your Life*. You get that one later. These are "How To" manuals. They are called *Getting By When You're Up The Creek Without a Paddle, Fighting Back When You're Sick of Getting Pushed Around, Love—What It is and How to Survive It*, or *How to Keep From Going Crazy When Everyone Around You Already Is*.

Obviously, sometime before you were born, your parents pawned the manuals for a down payment on a Chevy. Or maybe the tomes went overboard when *their* parents emigrated to America. Or were they incinerated during the big library fire in Alexandria?

Anyway, people keep fudging up replacements. You'll find them in the Philosophy section, the Psychology section, the Science section, and (Someone help you) the UFO Abduction/ Tarot/Astrology/Numerology section.

Look no further: you'll find the closest thing to the Lost Manuals in the science fiction section: the author was Robert A. Heinlein.

An engineer by trade, Heinlein knew that while machines can be duplicated, people can't be: no set of engineering instructions could apply to several billion individuals. He gave basic working diagrams; folks would have to jury-rig things from there.

Heinlein wrote fiction because that's what non-engineers could understand best—and he set his stories in strange lands because things were changing so fast that any land we encounter was *bound* to be.

Take the Lost Manual titled *Getting By When You're Up the Creek Without a Paddle*. Heinlein wrote several versions, each with a different slant. In *Tunnel in the Sky* teenagers on a two-week survival test find themselves stranded on a virgin planet, probably for good. In *Job: A Comedy of Justice* a preacher on vacation finds that while God might not play dice with the universe, it's only because He prefers *other* games.

In *Citizen of the Galaxy* a boy is sold into slavery to a crippled beggar ... and eventually concludes this was the *best* thing that ever happened to him. And in *Have Space Suit—Will Travel* a high school senior *is* abducted by a UFO, and ultimately finds himself in a distant courtroom appointed Clarence Darrow for the entire human race; this novel comes close to combining all the Lost Manuals into one.

Love—What It Is and How to Survive It: Heinlein wrote this several times, also. In *The Door Into Summer* a poor inventor lives through his fiancee turning into as much fun after work as Lucrezia Borgia; cryonics and a time machine give him a second shot at love. Time travel also helps Lazarus Long in *Time Enough For Love* find love a second time. It takes him 23 centuries to find the woman of his dreams but it turns out to be his own mother. (See previous Manual.)

As for *How to Keep from Going Crazy When Everyone Around You Already Is*—Heinlein considered most people "candidates for protective restraint." *Stranger in a Strange Land* is Heinlein's best attempt here. But try figuring out which characters aren't *already* crazy.

Fighting Back When You're Sick of Getting Pushed Around was Heinlein's favorite topic. His early novel *If This Goes On—*, included in *The Past Through Tomorrow*, has a preacher combining the worst of Pat Robertson, Jimmy Swaggart, and Orel Roberts elected president; a century later a Masonic Cabal is taking on the American theocracy run by the Prophet Incarnate. *Methuselah's Children* (also in *TPTT*) has Lazarus Long's tribe fleeing Earth to escape genocide.

Heinlein wrote four other novels of revolution. In *Sixth Column* super-science drives out the Pan-Asian conquerors of America. In *Red Planet* colonial rebels on Mars seek Martian help against absentee rulers on Earth. In *Between Planets* the rebellion stretches from Venus to Mars: this is my nomination for Robert A. Heinlein's best-written novel.

The Moon is a Harsh Mistress is Heinlein's libertarian classic—the *Atlas Shrugged* of science fiction. The revolution is on the moon; its leaders have read Ayn Rand; and one of them, Professor Bernardo de la Paz, is based on Heinlein's old buddy, Robert LeFevre of Rampart College.

Robert A. Heinlein, in his half-century career, wrote

over 45 books selling forty million copies worldwide. A mindful history will place him alongside Dickens and Twain.

We must cry that his pen has been set down for the last time: we can rejoice at the immense lost legacy he has regained for us.

A Letter to Joel Gotler

When Los Angeles literary agent, Joel Gotler, began representing Heinlein's film rights in 1986, Joel and I had been friends since he'd begun representing me eleven years earlier. Since that time, I'd also worked for Joel as an assistant on and off, got him started representing science fiction writers, which later became a substantial part of his "stable," and later co-represented several clients with him when I took my own shot at becoming a literary agent. So when I heard that Joel was taking on Heinlein as a client, I thought I'd better write him a "user's manual." So far, two of the novels I suggested for film submission — *Robert A. Heinlein's The Puppet Masters* and *Starship Troopers* — have been produced.

30 October 1986

Dear Joel:

I'm writing regarding your recent addition of Robert Heinlein to your client list. As you know, Vic Koman and I are both huge Heinlein fans. I've practically memorized Heinlein's entire writing output and have been a friend of the Heinleins since I interviewed Robert for the *New York Sunday News* in 1973. So I thought you might want some background by way of an introduction.

Heinlein was born July 7, 1907—which makes him just short of 80. He's a tough old bird who's a graduate of Annapolis, trained as an engineer, and served as a naval officer on aircraft carriers before World War Two until tuberculosis disabled him out. By the time World War Two broke out, he was already established as one of the top science fiction writers. He tried to get back into the navy for the war, but he was needed elsewhere, working as a civilian engineer for the military during the War.

After the War, Heinlein was the first American science fiction writer to break out of the pulps into the mass-market slick magazines—*Saturday Evening Post* for one—the first to have his science fiction novels published not only serialized in magazines but as *books*—and the first modern science fiction writer to have his work made into a successful movie: Heinlein co-scripted, and was technical consultant for George Pal's 1950 *Destination Moon*, based loosely on Heinlein's novel *Rocket Ship Galileo*—the huge success of which *started* the spate of science fiction movies of the 1950's. But Heinlein disliked working in Hollywood and after having his script for a 1951 picture called *Project Moonbase* turned into a mishmash by the producers, left Hollywood vowing never to return.

Heinlein's novel *Space Cadet* was the basis for both the *Space Cadet* TV series of the early 50's and the basis for the immensely popular *Tom Corbett—Space Cadet* series of books, which Heinlein didn't write but which a friend of his—scientist Willy Ley—acted as a consultant for. But *Space Cadet* has never been seriously filmed; it would be terrific.

For many years the Heinleins spent three quarters of each year traveling the world—both he and Ginny are multi-lingual—and one quarter of the year at home where he did his writing. Poor health in recent years (he had a stroke and carotid artery bypass in 1979) has interfered with that. Currently he suffers from emphysema and a troublesome nasal hemorrhage which recently has been hospitalizing him. But he's also vowed not to die until he can die on the moon. I hope he makes it and I wouldn't make large bets against it either.

After a decade of not writing much (only two novels in the 70's) he's been prolific recently—almost a book a year for the last few years. Heinlein never shows anybody *anything* until it's finished and never writes on contract, which he considers wage slavery. Ginny Heinlein has handled her husband's literary and business affairs for the last thirty or so years, and I've heard from writers and agents that she's a top expert on publishing, negotiating, and contracts—as good as the best agents in the business.

I should also mention that the Heinleins are hardcore libertarians. They're also supporters of Reagan's SDI "Star Wars" Defense program. (Heinlein was predicting the inevitability of space-based defenses as far back as the forties.) Incidentally, Heinlein is also the inventor of the water bed (the first manufacturer got the plans from Heinlein's description in *Stranger in a Strange Land*) and the robot arms used in radioactive labs are called "waldoes" after robot arms Heinlein first described in his 1940's story "Waldo."

Robert Heinlein is considered—by other leading lights in the field ranging from Isaac Asimov to Ray Bradbury to Jerry Pournelle and Larry Niven—as the most important science fiction writer since H.G. Wells and Jules Verne. I second or third the nomination. Half the ideas in modern science fiction—ideas that movies like *Star Wars* and E.T.—have made a fortune on—stem from one or another of Heinlein's books.

Twenty years before there was *E.T.*—about a human boy making friends with an alien—there was Heinlein's *The Star Beast*. The Force in *Star Wars* couldn't do anything that Heinlein's human raised by Martians, Valentine Michael Smith, didn't do first in *Stranger in a Strange Land*—and Luke Skywalker can trace his roots back to young heroes in Heinlein books like *Space Cadet* and *Starman Jones*. The book *Invasion of the Body Snatchers* came out about the same time as Heinlein's *The Puppet Masters*—but Heinlein's Puppet Masters are even more frightening than the Body Snatchers, and in *Puppet Masters* humans wage war against the planetwide invasion of alien slugs and *win*.

Aliens? Heinlein was there first, and better. Heinlein's *Starship Troopers* shows the training and combat of spaceborne Mobile Infantry fighting an interplanetary war against aliens a couple of centuries from now, and Heinlein's future marines—parachuting out of orbiting spaceships into alien cities, each man with more firepower than Patton's tank corps—are the toughest sons of bitches alive. Rambo probably would wash out of their training—he's too soft.

You want a Nick-and-Nora-type detective couple caught in a web of occult intrigue? Heinlein's novella *The Unpleasant Profession of Jonathan Hoag*. The ultimate paranoid fantasy about a man who's convinced the entire world is a charade put on for his benefit—

and it is? Heinlein's short story "They" is in that same volume.

An old billionaire has his brain transplanted into the body of his beautiful and accidentally-killed secretary? Heinlein's *I Will Fear No Evil* (1973).

The ultimate novel of interplanetary revolution and war with a computer, who makes HAL 9000 look stupid by comparison, organizing a moon-based revolution against Earth tyranny? *The Moon is a Harsh Mistress* (1966).

The ultimate post-nuclear holocaust novel? *Farnham's Freehold* (1964).

The life story of a 2,300-year-old man—born in 1912—which takes us two millennia into the future and across a couple of dozen planets? It also contains the best sequence about frontiering on another planet ever written. *Time Enough For Love* (1973).

You want *Star Wars*, *E.T.*, *Aliens*, and more all in one neat package? Heinlein was there first and best with *Have Space Suit—Will Travel*. Seventeen-year-old Kip Russell wins a space suit in a TV contest, fixes it up, is kidnaped out of his back yard by an alien spaceship full of creatures worse looking than *Alien*, and meets aboardship an 11-year-old girl who's a precocious genius and a friendly alien called The Mother Thing. The evil aliens are staging an invasion of earth, and Kip, the girl, and the Mother Thing have to stop them. The story takes Kip and friends on a dangerous moonwalk, into a dungeon on Pluto, and to an InterGalactic Court which will decide whether or not to destroy Earth because of our race's history of violence. This book is high adventure, high comedy, and serious philosophy all rolled together.

You want time travel that makes *Back to the Future* and *Peggy Sue Got Married* look like Edsels sitting next to a Ferrari? In *Time Enough For Love* the 2,000-year-old hero time-travels back to World War One, has an affair with his own mother, meets himself at five-years old, and enlists into the army for duty overseas. In Heinlein's *The Door Into Summer*, the hero is drugged and cryonically frozen by business enemies, awakens thirty years in the future, time-travels back thirty years to get even with his business enemies, and travels forward a second time to marry the little girl who fell in love with him in the past, time travel having resolved the age difference.

There's more: Heinlein has written over forty books—all still in print—and if there's a science fiction idea, Heinlein was probably there with it first and best.

[Some personal material deleted]

All best,

Neil

Copies: Robert & Virginia Heinlein
Victor Koman

Looking Upward Through the Microscope: Robert A. Heinlein

This is the article I wrote for the *New York Sunday News* in July, 1973, based on my interview with Heinlein. The *News* didn't publish it; *Reason* Magazine did, two years later.

In a letter to me, when I sent a copy of this to the Heinleins for their opinion, Virginia Heinlein said that Robert called it, "The best article—in style, content, and accuracy—of the many, many written about him over the years."

His devotees range from freaked-out astrologers to coolly rational astronomers; from Goldwater-country conservatives to Greenwich Village anarchists; from atheists such as Madalyn Murray O'Hair to members of the Church of All Worlds who proclaim him a prophet and his novel, *Stranger in A Strange Land*, a holy book.

Robert Heinlein's appeal knows no generation gap, spanning from his first story published in 1939 to his most recent bestseller, *Time Enough For Love*. Though he has written both novels aimed at adults and those for children, you'd be just as likely to find a doctoral candidate rereading one of his "juveniles" as you would to see a fifth-grader tackling one of his more advanced books for the first time. But as paradoxical as the sheer spectrum of readers he attracts is the man himself.

The unparalleled author of over 35 volumes of science fiction and adult fantasy, Robert Anson Heinlein is a fiery intellectual who feels as much at home with an anecdote as a syllogism. An indomitable individualist, he still believes the racial survival of humanity must be regarded as being of final importance. A devastating satirist of human society and government, he nonetheless prefers to keep silent about current politics.

His approach to life and literature is that of the field scientist: making observations and forming hypotheses. With this approach, combined with a style that invites the reader to draw up an asteroid and set a spell, Heinlein has influenced the development of modern science fiction more than any writer since H.G. Wells.

The most telling witness to his yarn-spinning abilities is that every book he's authored is still in print—this including stories that predict events now contradicted by reality. Even when his predictions have been dead wrong, when three decades of progress have turned what was thought to be hard scientific possibility into the improbabilities of fantasy, his stories still maintain a necessary ring of authenticity.

Prophetic

This shouldn't suggest that his ability to forecast the future had been any less than amazingly prophetic at times, though Heinlein stresses that prophecy as such is not the aim of science fiction. Nevertheless, in his 1941 novel, *Methuselah's Children*, he predicted a socially disoriented 1969 with such startling newspaper headlines as. "**LOS ANGELES HIGH SCHOOL MOB DEFIES SCHOOL BOARD**" and "**SUICIDE RATE UP NINTH SUCCESSIVE YEAR.**" Heinlein comments that nowadays such headlines don't even seem odd. His detailed description of the lunar surface in his 1947 juvenile novel, *Rocket Ship Galileo*, was accurate down even to the moon dust—and no one then knew whether moon dust even existed, or viewed it close up until the flight of *Apollo 11* twenty-two years later.

Much of his prophecy, however, has been of the self-fulfilling type. His fictional word "grok," used in *Stranger in A Strange Land* as a verb for total empathetic understanding, has been elevated to common usage. In his 1942 story, "Waldo," mechanical hands called waldoes were invented by the title character; when shortly thereafter such hands were actually developed to cope with highly radioactive materials, they were appropriately dubbed waldoes after those in the story. Heinlein designed a waterbed as far back as the 1930's but couldn't afford to build it then; he started using waterbeds in his fiction and now owns one sent to him as a compliment by the first man to manufacture them; he had gotten the idea from *Stranger in A Strange Land.*

But if writing prophecy is not Robert Heinlein's main intention, then what is?

"As far as I'm concerned, " Heinlein told this writer, "fiction is intended to entertain. If I can manage to entertain with it, that's what the cash customer is paying for. So I don't hesitate to write straight science fiction, straight fantasy, or a mixture of the two—or anything else."

What is science fiction, and how does it differ from fantasy?

"As you know, everybody takes a whack at that every now and then," said Heinlein. "Science fiction is, to my mind, based on the real world; extrapolation from the real world, speculation that takes place—usually into the future—about the real world, and which takes science as a necessary aspect of the story that you're writing—meaning if you left the science out the story would fall to pieces. Fantasy, on the other hand, is a fairy-tale for grown-ups. It is *not* based on the real world. This is no criticism of fantasy. I'm not opposed to it at all... I wrote both science fiction *and* fantasy and I sometimes mix them up in the same story in a way that purists do not like...but, sometimes you can tell a good story that way."

"I prefer the term 'speculative fiction,'" Heinlein continued, "because there isn't anything about *that* term which ties me down to putting a lot of atomic physics and such into a story. It's a *looser* term—more elbow room. Speculation about the future, but serious speculation."

Speculation

With speculations in mind, does Heinlein believe travel through time is possible, or is it merely a fictional device?

"There is no basis for belief or nonbelief in this question. We don't have any data from which to work. There is at present no satisfactory theory of time. We haven't the slightest idea of how you might get your teeth into the fabric of time—whatever it is. Time travel, as of now, comes under the head of fantasy, inasmuch as it requires one to postulate something about which we know nothing…But it makes an excellent device for telling stories, particularly stories that speculate about the condition of mankind and his future." Heinlein cited as classic examples of this type of story Mark Twain's *Connecticut Yankee in King Arthur's Court* and H.G. Wells' *Time Machine.*

Does Heinlein think any of the Unidentified Flying Objects have been actual contacts with beings from outer space?

"I don't know," he answered. "I simply don't have data. There have been some UFO sightings that are extremely hard to explain. I'm reminded of something Willy Ley said to me, oh, 20, 25 years ago. He said, "Vun. Dere is something dere. Two. I do not know vat it iss." I'm just about where Willy Ley put it then; there is something there and I do not know what it is."

In response to related questions, Heinlein added, "There have been lots of other writers who have always talked as if just as soon as we got in touch with really intelligent, highly advanced races, we will find them to be peaceful vegetarians. Well, I don't think that is necessarily true at all. There's no data on which to base that; it is simply wishful thinking on the part of the writers who write that way. The universe might turn out to be a hell of a sight nastier and tougher place than we have any reason to guess at this point. That first contact just *might* wipe out the human race, because we would encounter somebody who was meaner and tougher, and not at all inclined to be bothered by genocide. Be no more bothered by genocide than I am when I put out ant poison in the kitchen when the ants start swarming in."

Nonetheless Heinlein is definitely *not* preaching defeatism. "We got this way—we got where we are—over the course of a long stretch of evolution, by being survivor types in a very tough jungle. And from all I've seen of the human race so far, they're still that; mean, tough, and nasty. I do not mean that as a derogatory remark, either; I think that's what it takes to survive. That doesn't mean you have to be mean, tough, and nasty in your daily behavior. In other words I am not a pacifist, and I do not think the human animal is put together so he can be a pacifist and still survive."

Don't Tread On Me

Heinlein's views on government and individual freedom?

"I would say my position is not too far from that of Ayn Rand's; that I would like to see government reduced to no more than internal police and courts, external armed forces—with the other matters handled otherwise. I'm sick of the way the government sticks its nose into *every*thing, now...It seems to me that every time we manage to establish one freedom, they take another away. Maybe two."

But Robert Heinlein, being from Missouri, is careful not to represent any opinion as the final solution to any question. "I got over looking for final solutions," he explained, "a good, long time ago because once you get this point shored up, something breaks out somewhere else. The human race gets along by the skin of its teeth, and it's been doing so for some hundreds of thousands or millions of years. Human solutions are *never* final solutions, at least so far as the history of the race up to now indicates.

"When I was a kid we had the 'War to End All Wars'— going to make the world 'safe for democracy.' Now look at the damn thing...We thought we had all the problems of our economy solved except the problems of distribution...and now we suddenly discover that we're in a closed spaceship, a goldfish bowl, and if we don't get a balanced aquarium we're going to poison ourselves with our own poisons. It is the common human condition all through history that every time you solve a problem you discover that you've also created a new problem."

Intellectual surefootedness in the midst of an ever-changing universe is a prime requisite for sanity, and perhaps it is this quality that has earned Robert Heinlein so many devoted readers. Perhaps, however, his popularity can equally be traced to each of his stories being based on a postulate appealing to a different type of reader—though a substantial number of worshipful Heinlein fans have read all his published books. While Heinlein's stories have the nasty habit of being as difficult to label as Heinlein himself, some indications may be given as to which of his books appeals to what kind of reader.

Future History

His early stories (1939 to approx. 1950) might best be called "straight" science fiction or fantasy—depending on the particular story. Much of his science fiction during this period was included in what editors and publishers called his "Future History" series, though each story is complete unto itself. These include such titles *The Man Who Sold The Moon, The Green Hills of Earth, Revolt in 2100*, and *Methuselah's Children*. This last is particularly interesting as its main character, Lazarus Long, is also the protagonist of his latest novel, *Time Enough For Love*. Other of his science fiction novels worth noting from this period are *Orphans of the Sky* (tangentially part of the "Future History") and *Beyond This Horizon*, in which Heinlein deals directly with the question of "final answers." For some of his best fantasy from this period, see his two-in-one volume, *Waldo & Magic, Inc.*

Chronologically overlapping somewhat would be the dozen or so "juvenile" novels Heinlein wrote from about 1947 to 1958, though the juvenile categorization has much more to do with publishing industry traditions regarding youthful protagonists in fiction than literary treatment; most of Heinlein's novels so called are in no way juvenile. Among this writer's favorites are *Citizen of the Galaxy, Have Space Suit—Will Travel*, and *Between Planets*, with the rest just a short step behind. Favorite "adult" novels from this period include *The Puppet Masters, Double Star*, and his time travel novel, *The Door Into Summer*.

Starting with 1959 and *Starship Troopers*, Robert Heinlein's fiction has become ever more controversial with devotees sharply polarized in their favorites. Any attempt to pigeonhole novels of this period ends in chaos.

Stranger in A Strange Land (1961) awoke slowly to become an underground bestseller—must reading in college literary courses and communes—and remains one of Heinlein's all-time bestsellers. *Glory Road* is his 1963 science fantasy novel about a Vietnam veteran who meets a beautiful woman on *l'Île du Levant* and finds himself defending her in sword and sorcery combat. *The Moon is a Harsh Mistress* (1966) is regarded by some to be Heinlein's all-around best novel. It tells of the fight of a 21st century lunar colony to gain in political independence from earth; its antiauthoritarian overtones have won it wide popularity among libertarians and classical liberals.

New Approach

Both *I Will Fear No Evil* (1970) and *Time Enough For Love* (1973) represent a shift in emphasis in Heinlein's writings; more sex and philosophy, less fast-paced adventure. Heinlein comments: "Sex is so central an element in every human being and in the development of the human race that to have left it out of science fiction—as it was for many years—was a major fault in science fiction, and I'm very pleased that it's now possible to write about it... Human sexuality is so major a factor in the human race that any attempt to deal with the human race or with people realistically which *omits* this factor cannot really be a mature treatment. And yet I know there are people who would be made uneasy in some fashion if sex gets into it, and yet sex *has* to be in it if we're to have human beings.

For an author to explore new regions sometimes earns him harsh criticisms from fans who have liked previous works. "I never pay any attention to this," said Heinlein, "because it has been my intention—my purpose—to make every story I've written different from every other story I've written—never to write a story just like my last one."

And though he has been successful in this quest, every Heinlein story *does* have at least one thing in common with the others; each has the unmistakable imprint of the scientist-turned-minstrel who from under the microscope looks up at the most interesting specimens of all.

beHEIN the LEIN:

Robert Heinlein was born in Butler, Missouri on July 7, 1907 into a large family tracing it roots back to a Bavarian-German ancestor who emigrated to America in 1756. He was raised in Kansas City, Missouri, won an appointment to Annapolis where he was noted as a champion swordsman, and served as a line officer on destroyers and aircraft carriers for five years until being disabled out of the Navy. He started writing science fiction in 1938 "to pay off a mortgage" and within two years was regarded as one of the leaders in the field.

A widely traveled man of many interests and skills, Heinlein is an experienced research & development engineer in aircraft and high altitudes, as well as being a capable architect, mechanic, and construction worker. He is a lover of Chopin, chess, and contract bridge, the last two being "compelling time-takers" which he says he won't again have time for until he retires from writing—if ever.

He presently lives in a self-designed house outside Santa Cruz, California "which is circular because Mrs. Heinlein wanted a circular house." Virginia Heinlein is a biochemist specializing in the genetics of tropical plants, and is an amateur linguist who can speak eight languages.

Robert Heinlein has twice been Guest of Honor at World Science Fiction Conventions (1941 and 1961) and he will again be Guest of Honor at the 1976 Worldcon to be held in his hometown of Kansas City. Four of Heinlein's novels have won the coveted Hugo award given out by the World SF Conventions (an unmatched record), and this past April, the professional organization of the field, the Science Fiction Writers of America, made Heinlein the first and so far only recipient of its Grand Master Nebula Award for a lifetime of outstanding achievement in the science fiction genre.

Rumor has it that Mr. Heinlein has started work on yet another novel, and Berkeley Books has released his entire "Future History" in one paperback volume for the first time under the title, *The Past Through Tomorrow*.

Revolt in 2100

Reviewed by J. Neil Schulman

1972

Revolt in 2100 contains three stories, all from Robert Anson Heinlein's earliest significant body of work, his "Future History" series. Two of these stories, "If This Goes On—" (a novel) and "Coventry" (a novella) are among the most libertarian he has ever penned, and well worth reexamining for those in search of literature expressing our ideals. The third story, a short one entitled "Misfit," has no great significance to the libertarian, and I will therefore dispense entirely with it for the purposes of this review.

"If This Goes On—" is Heinlein's very first novel and unlike so many first novels, is still eminently readable over thirty years after it was written. Written in the late 1930's, and according to Richard Friedman partially inspired by Sinclair Lewis's *It Can't Happen Here* (something I can not verify from personal knowledge), the most remarkable feature of "If This Goes On—" is perhaps its many similarities to one of Heinlein's most recent (and perhaps most libertarian) novel, *The Moon is a Harsh Mistress*. This is a point I will elaborate on shortly.

In about the year 2075 A.D. (contrary to the "2100" in the book's title, and remarkably the exact same year as the revolution in *The Moon is a Harsh Mistress*), the United States is in the midst of a new, but somehow highly technological, Dark Ages, under the thumb of a theocratic dictator called "The Prophet Incarnate."

The story opens told first person by John Lyle, a "legate" fresh out of West Point, and a guardsman in the Angels of the Lord, the personal guard to the Prophet. While standing guard outside the Prophet's personal quarters one night, Lyle meets Sister Judith, a "Holy Deaconess" in the personal service of the Prophet, that is, she's one of his "virgins." Sister Judith is even more recently arrived at the Prophet's palace than is Lyle, and consequently has not yet had the "honor" to serve the Prophet personally, and she is too naive to know what this service will entail. John Lyle and Sister Judith see each other for several other brief moments around the palace, then exactly one month after their original encounter, their "shifts" meet up again, and Lyle is standing outside the Prophet's apartments when Sister Judith is called for her first "service." A few minutes later when she finds out, she screams making a big scene, and is sent back to her cell to repent.

Lyle asks his older, palace/politics-wise roommate, Zeb Jones, what the commotion was about, and upon finding out, swears that he must rescue Sister Judith. Jones agrees to help, for reasons of his own, and consequently the two of them are sworn in as members of the Cabal, a revolutionary organization which is planning the overthrow of the Prophet's dictatorship, and a return to the former U.S. republic.

The plot develops, Sister Judith is rescued, and Lyle and Jones, no longer able to function in secrecy at the palace, are transferred to the revolution's huge and beautifully-equipped secret headquarters. The rest of the story involves Lyle's reorientation to a free-thinking man, and his personal account of the revolution.

There are many points Heinlein brings out in this story which he was to also emphasize in *The Moon is a Harsh Mistress*, ideas such as: revolution is Big Business but necessarily carried out by amateurs; every revolution is a unique event; revolutionary action requires a well-manned, well-financed operation, etc., etc. There are also similarities in the way Heinlein deals with his characters: remember the way Prof dies after his big speech in *The Moon is a Harsh Mistress*? Well, in "If This Goes On—" an old man, looking somewhat like Mark Twain, according to Heinlein, makes a highly libertarian speech and then promptly drops dead.

It would seem to me from these similarities that Heinlein's return to early themes is perhaps a sign that this overall political orientation is not that markedly different than from his early writing days—or if it is, you couldn't tell it from his fiction.

In "Coventry," Heinlein brings out the main principle explicitly that differentiates libertarians from every other political philosophy. "No possible act, nor mode of conduct, was forbidden to you, as long as your action did not damage another. Even an act specifically prohibited by law could not be held against you, unless the state was able to prove that your act damaged, or caused evident danger of damage, to a particular individual..."

This speech is given by a judge in Heinlein's libertarian society, the outcome of the successful revolution in "If This Goes On—", to David Mackinnon, a young, impetuous man who is charged with punching someone in the nose for verbally insulting him. Since physical violence is the one thing forbidden in this society, Mackinnon is sentenced to choose between the Two Alternatives: either he submits to psychological reorientation to correct his wish to damage others, or he will be sent to Coventry, a section of the United States which the new society has set aside for those persons who wish not to accept the social contract of not damaging others. Coventry is inescapable, and the government completely withdraws itself from those who desire to enter it.

Mackinnon enters Coventry, in the belief that he will find a "frontier anarchy," but what he finds instead is that the territory has been divided into three separate states, one, an absolute dictatorship, one, a continuation of the theocracy of "If This Goes On—", Prophet Incarnate and all, and the third, in which he finds himself, a corrupt and repressive republic not unlike our own. The story revolves about his reorientation to understand the necessity of the non-intervention doctrine, and his subsequent agreement to return to the outside world and accept the ban on force.

The main fault of "Coventry," of course, is that Heinlein did not realize the market's ability to provide protection against aggression. The mistake is also made by the absence of any reference to attempted restitution to the victim of aggression for any damage or deprivation caused him; and a recognition of the principle that punching a man in the nose is not grounds to remove a man from his property. It might also be objected that "psychological orientation" is an unessential issue, as long as a person understands the consequences of violating someone else's rights.

All in all, these stories are well written, highly enjoyable, and I would recommend *Revolt in 2100* to anyone desiring a valuable addition to their libertarian library.

Time Enough For Love: The Lives of Lazarus Long

Reviewed by J. Neil Schulman

This is the review which I sold to The New York Times Book Review *in 1973, minus irrelevant material about another book not by Heinlein.* The New York Times *killed the review ... but by doing so inadvertently made it possible for me to meet Heinlein.*

Immortality has long been fair game only to the science fiction author or earlier equivalents, therefore it shouldn't surprise anyone when its most revered living practitioner chooses to return to the subject.

In *Methuselah's Children*, a novel from his "Future History" series written mostly in the 'forties, Robert A. Heinlein introduced Lazarus Long, the oldest and most curmudgeonly member of the Howard Families, a clan of humans that scientific inbreeding had given a lifespan of several times the norm. *Time Enough For Love*, his eagerly-anticipated latest novel, returns to the "Future History" series—though familiarity with it isn't necessary to enjoyment of this new book—by chronicling Lazarus Long's activities over twenty-three centuries of life.

In 4272 on Secundus, a planet owned entirely by Lazarus Long and populated mostly by his descendants, Lazarus has been imprisoned in a rejuvenation hospital by a descendent, Ira Weatheral, Chairman Pro-Tem of the Howard Families (Lazarus's status as Senior Member makes him Chairman at will), after Lazarus attempts to bypass rejuvenation and die peacefully: he is bored and wishes to die.

His indomitable will temporarily foiled, the "Senior" offers a deal: he will agree to Weatheral's request that he complete rejuvenation and dictate his entire memoirs if Weatheral can find something *new* for him to do; if he fails, Lazarus is to be allowed to suicide. Weatheral agrees.

The ensuing chronicle is not a single, consistent narrative, but several interconnecting ones, comprising first and third person expositions, lengthy stretches of conversation, notebooks (meditations), all supposedly compiled and edited by the Howard Archivist Emeritus. In this, his longest, most ambitious, and most mature novel in a career studded with masterpieces, Heinlein examines virtually every aspect of the human experience, from war, peace, religion, slavery, pioneering, gangsterism, and a host of sexual practices, to several experiences unique to science fiction. Perhaps the most revealing statement about his goal in this novel could have been made by Heinlein himself in an interview published in *Oui* Magazine in December, 1972: "A novel—which is what I've been writing in recent years—if it's to be a real novel and not simply an extended short story, necessarily takes in the human condition, and if you don't think the human condition as a whole is in fairly bad shape at the moment, take a look around you."

A Heinlein fan accustomed to his tightly-constructed, adventure stories of the 'forties and 'fifties may be somewhat disappointed by the leisurely pace and muted philosophic tone Heinlein takes in *Time Enough For Love*, but it is perhaps this stylistic departure that signals Heinlein's emergence in the 'seventies as a speculator into humanity's soul, as well as its purely external progress. But where else can a serious science fiction writer go when he has seen speculations ridiculous fifteen years ago transformed into fact—indeed, even being outstripped by reality itself?

Letter to *Prometheus*

1983

The following letter was published in the Summer, 1983 issue of *Prometheus*, the newsletter of the Libertarian Futurist Society, the organization which gives out the Prometheus Award, of which Heinlein and I are both recipients (thought I wasn't at the time I wrote this letter). It was sparked by comments Greg Costikyan had made in the previous issue in his review of Heinlein's novel, *Friday*, which was a nominee for the award. (It didn't win.) My letter was not so much a reply to Costikyan's review as it was a comment on certain assumptions Costikyan was making about Heinlein based on books by Alexei Panshin and H. Bruce Franklin, and as such doesn't require a reading of Costikyan's review to gain the context.

Just a LOC (Letter Of Comment, for those of you who don't speak fannish) on Greg Costikyan's review of *Friday*.

Being a fan of Heinlein's for as long as I can remember (I must have started reading him as early as nine or ten), I was one of the first people to get Alexei Panshin's *Heinlein in Dimension*, and I drank in what Panshin said about my literary hero. I thought so well of the book that I recommended it to Heinlein when I first spoke to him back in July, 1973, an interview that I conducted with Heinlein for the *New York Sunday News*, which that paper bought and paid for, but which ended up being published instead in *Reason* and *New Libertarian Notes* in different forms.

In the course of that interview, however, and subsequently in further conversations with Heinlein, I have come to the conclusion that Panshin just didn't know what he was talking about a lot of the time.

Let me illustrate. Panshin talks about how Heinlein was repressed about sex in his early fiction. I don't have the book in front of me so I can't give an exact quote, but there's something about Heinlein having a Boy Scout's view of sexuality. In fact what Panshin was noting was the repressive editorial *standards* that restricted what Heinlein could publish in the science-fiction pulps and the Scribners' line of juvenile books. Given a Kay Tarrant, John Campbell's assistant at *Astounding*, who would systematically go through each manuscript and cut out *anything* that was even vaguely sexual, I find it astonishing that Heinlein managed to get in as *much* as he did in his early works.

The same sort of sloppy research and thinking can be found in H. Bruce Franklin's booklet on Heinlein. The charges of racism in *Sixth Column* and *Farnham's Freehold* are both vile and absurd to anyone familiar with Heinlein's personal attitudes. He is, and has always been, an individualist, no matter what else his political views were and are. In *Sixth Column* which Heinlein wrote from an outline by John Campbell and of which he says in *Expanded Universe* he didn't want to write and still doesn't like very much, Heinlein goes out of his way to treat the Pan-Asian conquerors of America as villains because of *their* racism, and pointedly makes an American of Asian extraction a sympathetic and heroic character.

And in *Farnham's Freehold*, Heinlein makes the most powerful and uncompromising attack on racism that I have found *anywhere*. The book is a role reversal where in a future post-nuclear-holocaust Earth whites are the slaves of blacks, and the role-reversal is complete down to every nuance. Whites are lazy and servile; blacks are supercilious, show king's mercy to emphasize their superiority, and treat whites as animals.

This is not the first time I have heard the charge of racism against Heinlein: I also heard it from Samuel R. Delaney in a speech he made at the University of Colorado in 1981. Delaney was and is wrong, and frankly I expect better criticism from a man of his talents. Heinlein was not putting us on when he said that *Stranger in a Strange Land* and *Starship Troopers* both make exactly the same statement about humanity. Both show individuals who are willing to sacrifice themselves for the sake of humanity.

Here, if anywhere, is where *I* have a fundamental disagreement with Heinlein, but one which I think is peripheral to much of his literary intent. But let me get this into print for once. Heinlein stated to me, in our 1973 conversation, and goes into detail in *Expanded Universe*, that the highest morality consists of the individual who is willing to give up his life for the sake of his family, village, or nation, and, ultimately, the survival of his species. (He also goes out of his way to make clear that he considers this is a choice which must be made voluntarily by each individual; no collective has the right to demand this as a duty.)

Where I disagree is that I value the individual above any concept of a collective. I don't see any gain for a family, village, nation, or species that survives by the sacrifice of its best individuals.

Mind you, I can well see selling my life to buy the lives of people I dearly love: parents, sister, children, wife, friend. But it would be a choice made for individuals I *love*, not "others" in some abstract sense. To paraphrase Rand, if the future of the human species demands the sacrifice of the best of the present, then the future of the human species be damned.

The only rational case I can see for placing the value of others above one's own life is the case argued by Christianity: love of all mankind. If one does, in fact, love all mankind as brothers, then sacrificing one's own life for them is a good bargain. It's a choice that people argue that Jesus made, and history provides other examples with better evidence of many people who are willing to sacrifice their own lives for the sake of a greater good. But let me point out here that Christianity offers a specific value to the individual for that sacrifice which, to my knowledge, Heinlein's stated metaphysics does not: those who love others well enough to give up their lives for them *live forever.* This is an appeal I can understand, and if I were convinced this were true, it would seem to me to be the best offer I've ever had.

Lacking conviction on this point, I don't see why others *per se* are of such ultimate value. They, too, will eventually die. (Yes, even if the human race expands into space, the human race will eventually die, either by changing into something non-human, or by the death of the universe itself, whenever that happens.)

So I remain an uncompromising individualist, and when Heinlein focuses on *this* aspect of his values, I applaud and will continue applauding.

This is, perhaps, much too heavy for what started out as a simple letter in reply to a book review, but inasmuch as it deals with values necessary to evaluate perhaps the most central aspects of Heinlein's libertarianism, I hope I will be forgiven.

This said, to *Friday* itself. I do not intend ever again to go into print with an opinion on Heinlein's current fiction. I find the task of critical review an obstruction to my own enjoyment of a writer's work. So without any evaluation of whether Heinlein's intent is good or bad, let me just say that I would think Heinlein circa the 1950's would have executed this book differently than Heinlein circa 1981. In *Citizen of the Galaxy*, when Baslim dies Thorby is given explicit instructions on how he is to carry on and he decides, specifically, to carry on Baslim's work. In *Friday*, when Friday's mentor dies, she is left completely at loose ends, and the work as abandoned as hopeless.

This reflects, in my view, a shift in Heinlein's emphasis from an optimistic view of life to a pessimistic view. Whether Heinlein is convinced of this, or whether he is simply trying to scare us in getting out into space, I can't guess. But I don't think anyone needs to develop any elaborate theories about the stages of Heinlein's career to explain the change of direction in his fiction.

I have just one question for Greg Costikyan: why bother with the opinions of the Panshins and Franklins—

and, yes, the Schulmans for that matter—when Heinlein is perfectly capable of explaining what he's up to in his *own* words, and has done so in detail in *Expanded Universe*?

J. Neil Schulman,
Long Beach, California

Addendum, 1990: As the review of *Job: A Comedy of Justice*, later in this book, demonstrates, my intent not to review any more of Heinlein's "current fiction" didn't last long. But I had bought *Job* for my own enjoyment, and read it twice already, when the request to review it came in from *New Libertarian*. Inasmuch as I knew it would be an overwhelming positive review, I didn't suffer any loss of enjoyment reviewing it.—JNS

A Letter to Virginia and Robert Heinlein

21 August 1984

Dear Ginny & Robert:

As you can see from the letterhead, I'm visiting my folks in San Antonio this summer while working on my next novel; but I'll be back in Southern California for at least a few days, some good news being the reason: I've just been told that *The Rainbow Cadenza* has won the Prometheus Award for 1984, and inasmuch as it will be given in a ceremony at the LA Worldcon, I will be flying back to accept it. (My mother will be flying with me, my father being unable to attend because of the beginning of the symphony season here.) And while I'm not expecting to see you there, if perchance you *are* going to be in the neighborhood, the ceremony will be at the L.A.Con (at the Anaheim Convention Center and surrounding hotels) on Friday, August 30th, at 6:00 PM.

Having gotten the patting-myself-on-the-back out of the way, the rest of this letter will be a LOC on *Job: A Comedy of Justice*, which my mother saw in the window display of a Waldenbooks while we were shopping yesterday, which I immediately rushed in and bought, and which I spent yesterday evening and this morning reading, cover-to-cover.

Robert, you and I have known each other, now, for about ten years—and I think it's time you leveled with me. I'm sure you've noticed, whenever we've been in the same room together, that I have a tendency to stare at you. That's because I've always had a suspicion that you're not what you seem to be, and I've been watching closely for your persona to slip, for just an instant, so I can catch you out.

Well, I'm afraid you've clinched it in my mind this time. Having written a couple of novels myself, now, it has become pretty obvious to me what *is* and *is not* possible for an author to do using mundane methods— and it is *not* possible for an ordinary human being to have written as intelligent, perceptive, and funny a metaphysical speculation as *Job*.

So, fess up. This Midwestern Boy act of yours just won't cut it any more. Which *Earth* were you born on? Dirigibles or airplanes? Was it really 1907—as you claim—or more likely 3207? I assume too much. Was it even *Earth*?

I must admit, you have everyone fooled—but not me. Remember, when I first interviewed you, I asked—just to make sure—whether you were able to write the memoirs of Lazarus Long because you were approaching your own second millennium? And you said, "Neil, I'm not even a hundred, yet." You said it so *sincerely* you almost had me believing you. But not any more. I also asked what you knew about UFO's. You said, "I don't have any data." What does that mean: that the requirements of your mission here on Earth require you to keep nothing on file that we Earthlings might get our hands on?

What a cover! A science fiction writer. Who could

possibly believe that you've been writing fact, not fancy, for the last 45 years? You've even made a couple of deliberate errors in prediction (but not many) just to throw everyone off the track.

But you're not fooling me anymore. People born and bred on this planet just don't *think* as well as you do. Listen, I'm not stupid, and you had several dozen major challenges to traditional human thought in *Job*—some I never even came *close* to thinking of.

Have you met the Glaroon?

Are you the Glaroon?

One caution, though. You've written often enough about the dangers to the monkey which has been dyed pink, when placed back in among the brown monkeys. I'm afraid this time you've exposed yourself, once and for all. So, in the name of the Chairman, *be careful.* I might *not* be the only one who's seen through your cover.

Best,
Neil

Job: A Comedy of Justice
Reviewed by J. Neil Schulman

1985

Anybody who knows me at all knows that there are three authors I revere above all others—Ayn Rand, C.S. Lewis, and Robert Heinlein.

There are other writers of whom I stand in awe for specific qualities. I consider Anthony Burgess to be the best English prose stylist I've ever encountered—*A Clockwork Orange*, in particular, astounds me for its use of language. Ira Levin knocks me silly with his masterful integration of descriptive detail into story-telling. J.D. Salinger and John Irving reach directly into my heart and squeeze: Holden Caulfield and Garp are characters I would have for friends if I ever met them; both Salinger and Irving, also, are stylistic masters. Colin Wilson can take a subject as dreary to me as vampires and turn it into a fascinating look at psycho-sexuality.

All these—and other—writers, I admire as stylists, thinkers, and story-tellers. But what makes me pick out Rand, Lewis, and Heinlein—and set them apart from other authors—is that these three are the writers who have been battling for my soul.

Lewis, Heinlein, and Rand converted me to rationalism.

Heinlein and Rand converted me to libertarianism.

All three have made me an arch-romantic and stern

optimist.

Because of these three writers, I wrote my first two novels.

Lewis converted me from atheism to Christianity—Rand converted me back to atheism, with Heinlein standing on the sidelines rooting for agnosticism. Then I put the argument into the mouths of my own characters in *The Rainbow Cadenza* and found Lewis winning the battle for my soul again.

Damned if I know where it'll end up.

I never met Lewis—he died the year I first picked up one of his *Narnia Chronicles*. I managed to meet Rand on the telephone: I argued with her for hours, and found her mind to be even more stunningly cogent in conversation than it was in print. But the woman was so bitter and ungiving that I could hardly believe this was the same radiant spirit I'd met on the pages of *Atlas Shrugged*.

Then, Heinlein. Boy, things get complicated there. After being an avid fan of his since nine or ten years old, I first met him at age 20 in 1973. I learned that he's the same man in person that you meet through his books. I interviewed him for hours, once commissioned an original piece of art as a gift for him, followed him around New York City one day like a puppy dog, made the biggest blunder of my literary career while trying to get him to endorse *Alongside Night*, was his stentor at his reception for blood-donors, and named a torchship for him in *Rainbow Cadenza*.

I feel like a private being inspected by a general

whenever I talk to him. I'm always afraid I'll say something stupid and because I'm so nervous, half the time I do. I see the man the way I see my own father: my father's life as a virtuoso violinist is a symbol to me of the necessity of pursuing supreme excellence and the possibility of achieving it—Robert Heinlein taught me how to take that symbol and apply it to my own life.

Which brings us to last August, when Heinlein's new novel *Job: A Comedy of Justice* showed up in the window display of a Waldenbooks. I ran in and bought a copy, interrupting my own writing to read the new Heinlein. And I read it practically in one sitting.

Now, I may be accused of being prejudiced because I think virtually everything Heinlein has written has one thing or another that makes it worth reading, but this time—regardless of what you may think about books like *I Will Fear No Evil, Starship Troopers*, and *The Number of the Beast*—for which Heinlein has gotten heat—this time, Heinlein has really outdone himself.

Job is great.

In a nutshell, *Job* is a travelogue through multiple parallel-Earths (an s-f or fantasy story, depending on your own metaphysics) in which its first-person hero, Alex, and heroine, Margrethe, never stay in any place long enough to do more than get familiar with some new history books before they're facing still another Earth. The book ultimately takes us through a dozen alternate histories of Earth, then through Heaven and Hell, then even-more bizarre places.

Job is as good as anything Heinlein has written and

better than anything except possibly *Stranger in a Strange Land* or *The Moon is a Harsh Mistress*. It is hysterically funny, brilliantly inventive, well-plotted, well-paced, romantic, and stylishly executed.

(And, parenthetically, it is a sequel-of-sorts to two other Heinlein stories: his novella *The Unpleasant Profession of Jonathan Hoag* and his short story, "They"— though *Job* contains only one brief reference to "The Glaroon" from the latter and the "sequelness" to "Jonathan Hoag" exists only in identical metaphysics.)

Would you believe that Heinlein can take Alex, a bigoted, Bible-Belt, anti-libertarian fundamentalist ex-preacher, and make him a sympathetic hero? (You can deduce, however, that this is a man-who-learns-better story.)

And that this guy falls in love with Margrethe, a beautiful Odin-worshipper, and has to try saving *her* soul?

But, to me at least, *Job*'s real interest lies not in its characters and story, but in its theological and doctrinal underpinnings. This is probably the most irreligious s-f novel published in the English language since Michael Moorcock's *Behold the Man*—or you might have to go back to Mark Twain's *Connecticut Yankee in King Arthur's Court*. (This definition carefully excludes Victor Koman's equally irreligious novel, *The Jehovah Contract*, soon to be published for the first time in a German-language translation, but yet to be published in the prophet's homeland or native tongue.)

C.S. Lewis would have cringed (after he stopped

laughing) at Heinlein's portrayals of Heaven: a class-conscious Bureaucracy where Angels are first-class citizens and saved humans ride in the back-of-the-bus—it's got good architecture and the best hamburgers to be found anywhere, but no decent libraries; Hell: a benevolent Principality run by Lucifer, the Prince of Darkness, as a benevolent anarchocapitalist society, and the hotel service beats anything in Heaven; Jehovah: a pettish young Jewish artist; and Lucifer: Jehovah's brother—and the nicer of the two. But you can't assume from this lack of respect to religion that *Job* is a book Ayn Rand would have liked.

If Lewis was in fiction the best Twentieth Century apologist of Christianity, and Rand in fiction was the best Twentieth Century advocate of Objectivism, then—in *Job*—Heinlein has firmly established himself as the best advocate of the "The Universe Isn't Anything Like You Bastards Have Even Been Able To Imagine" school of metaphysics. The man makes the paranoia in *Illuminatus!* look tame by comparison.

Now I'm going to do something that Heinlein says he doesn't mean his readers to do: take him seriously. Heinlein says he's in the business of writing entertainments for cash, not in the business of making philosophical statements. Undoubtedly, this saves him from a lot of arguments, particularly from people like me, who love to argue philosophy.

But, I said earlier that Heinlein is in battle with Lewis and Rand for my soul, and it is that aspect of *Job* that I want to address.

I'm not a Biblical expert, so I can hardly comment on what relationship there is between the Biblical character of Job and Heinlein's character of Alex, who is supposed to be a second Job. But I find it a little easier to comment on the character of God as He appears in Heinlein as compared to Lewis. (Rand is out of this particular argument—she wouldn't have deigned to debate it.)

C.S. Lewis, in his belief and advocacy of Christianity, takes the Judeo-Christian tradition at its word: Jehovah is the First Cause, creator of all that isn't Himself, the primary Fact of Existence and Consciousness Together—that which Was, Is, and Always Shall Be—the Creator of the Angels before He created Man. Lucifer was merely an Angel who abused his free will and chose Evil: the equivalent power not of God, but of Michael.

Heinlein portrays Jehovah and Lucifer as brothers—equivalent in power as only two of many Gods—both of whom are subservient to a still Higher Power—a God even to Jehovah—whom Heinlein calls "The Chairman, Mr. Koshchei." The name has been used before elsewhere, by James Branch Cabell for the Bureaucrat who runs the Universe, and as the Magician in Igor Stravinsky's 1911 ballet *Petrushka*.

In effect, by demoting Jehovah to a rank equivalent to Lucifer, Heinlein has portrayed in *Job* that He Who C.S. Lewis worshipped as God is merely (in Lewis's terms) an Angel—and a dishonest, megalomaniacal, and cruel one at that. God is another level up.

What Lewis might properly have asked at this point (if he took Heinlein's fantasy at its word) is: (A) what evidence Heinlein or anyone else could have in suggesting this possibility; and: (B) if Koshchei is, after all, God, then wouldn't prayers directed to Our Father in Heaven go not to Koshchei's deceitful angel Jehovah, but to Koshchei?

Even if he doesn't want to be taken seriously, Heinlein tries to answer at least some of the theological questions raised by his paradigm, much of his explanation out of the mouth of the most sympathetic character in the story—Lucifer. Unfortunately, the so-called Prince of Lies keeps contradicting himself.

Lucifer explains to Alex that Koshchei has no desire to be worshipped, and tells Alex that in saying to Jehovah, "Thy will be done," Alex is setting himself up for any sadism that Jehovah can think up—"the test of Job."

Then, in the only case we see that Lucifer is being judged by Koshchei—involving the possibility of Lucifer being sent to a *real* hell of sorts (see Heinlein's story, "They" for the exact nature of this threatened banishment) Lucifer tells Koshchei, "I must leave it to the Chairman's judgment." And Koshchei replies, "Yes, you must."

As for me, I see no semantic difference between "Thy Will Be Done" and "I must leave it to Your Judgment."

Lucifer also goes to great length to tell Alex that justice is a human illusion—then goes out of his way to prove himself a Just Being. Lucifer sticks his neck way out for Alex—a creature far below himself from which he can gain nothing—telling Koshchei at great personal risk that, "[T]his animal ... tried hard on my behalf when it believed me to be in extreme danger. Now that it is in trouble I owe it an equal effort."

A Being who acts on such a Principle of Reciprocity, for all his protestations, believes in Justice.

Then, *Koshchei* punishes Jehovah for his treatment of Mankind, saying, "Aren't you the God who announced the rule concerning binding the mouths of the kine that tread the grain?" And Justice is supposed to be a human illusion? Hah!

But one moment in Heinlein's portrayal of Koshchei would have given even C.S. Lewis pause: one, single image of Koshchei's True Face seems to create the Awe that Lewis was talking about, the *sehnsucht* that caused his belief in God.

Alex, narrating, tells us, "I looked into that great face; Its eyes held me. They got bigger, and bigger, and bigger. I slumped forward and fell into them."

Job may be anti-religious. But it's hardly anti-Supreme Deity.

Ultimately, however, Heinlein's paradigm cannot be taken seriously—exactly as Heinlein would wish—since it is published only as fiction. Lewis claimed that his portrayals of God (as Aslan in *Narnia*, as Maleldil in the *Ransom* trilogy) were actual attempts to portray, as best he could understand it, a Being whom he believed actually exists.

Rand, while not believing that her perfect man John

Galt existed apart from his appearance in ink on paper, believed that the qualities she portrayed in Galt were achievable in reality.

Robert A. Heinlein makes no claim whatsoever, aside from his hope that the $16.95 plus tax that the hardcover set me back entertained me enough that I'll plunk down again for his next book.

I will, Sir, I will. But, really, is it hoping too much that someday you'll go on the record—as Lewis and Rand have—with your thoughts on what sort of universe(s) you think we're *really* in?

The
Robert Heinlein
Interview

Introduction
or
The Giant *Chutzpah* Strikes Again

There I was sitting at my typewriter doing a fifth rewrite on my review of *Time Enough For Love* and wondering what He would think, when suddenly the telephone rang and He said, "This is Robert Heinlein. May I speak to Mr. J. Neil Schulman?"

Perhaps I'd better back up just a bit.

When I was ten and living in Natick, Massachusetts (pop. approx. 25,000), my fourth grade class was escorted to the Morse Institute Library—the children's division, upstairs—on the first of regular, monthly visits. Once there, we were released into our own custody with nothing more than an admonition to rendezvous back at the door (in double file, or course) with whatever books we wanted.

At that age I was an addict of *Superman* comics (I'd have found his ability to fly quite useful in evading my relentless antagonists—the little beasts!) and I suppose that was one of the factors that drew me over to the science fiction. I took out either *Rocket Ship Galileo* or *Red Planet* that first time—I can't remember which; in any case, by the end of the term I was a confirmed Heinlein addict as well.

Which was one of the few good breaks I had in an otherwise rotten childhood.

(It might be instructive to here recall Dr. Thomas Szasz's definition of childhood as a twenty year prison term.)

By the time I finished elementary school I'd read not only all Heinlein's "juveniles" but also whatever books of his were carried in the downstairs adult library—a joyous discovery when I learned that my favorite author also wrote books for grown-ups.

I was just about convinced I'd read every book Heinlein had written when a fellow cadet in the Civil Air Patrol told me about a science fiction book, "with all this sex in it, see?" It turned out to be *Stranger in a Strange Land*, of course, and I realized that the prim librarians at Morse Institute hadn't noticed anything written after *Starship Troopers*. After which, with the aid of paperback bookstores, I soon *had* read virtually every book he'd written.

If you wish a psycho-philosophical explanation of why I responded so strongly to Heinlein's writings, I suggest you turn to Ayn Rand's *Romantic Manifesto*; I have no wish to delve into such esoterics here. Suffice that his fiction instilled in me a deep respect for science, intelligence, competence, autonomy, liberty, and all-around horse sense, as well as being one of the few links to a sane value-orientation I had in those God-forsaken years.

Then on January 10, 1971 through no fault of his own, Robert Heinlein turned me on to libertarianism.

My mother, a diehard *New York Sunday Times* cross-word-doer, said to me, "Hey your favorite author's picture is in the *Times Magazine*." (She has severely regretted doing so ever since.) I rushed over and sure enough there it was—but who were all these strangers in the pictures around him: Ayn Rand, Murray Rothbard, Jerome Tuccille, Karl Hess, Baruch Spinoza? (Spinoza??!!) I read the article entitled "The New Right Credo—Libertarianism" by Stan Lehr and Louis Rossetto Jr.*, and said to myself, "So *that's* what the set-up in 'Coventry' is all about." Ten months later I had started the Borough of Manhattan Community College Libertarian Coalition and the rest is history; I kept on in Libertarian activities until I reached my present pre-eminence in the movement. (Ouch! That's initiation of force, Sam...)

As to how this interview came about.

Being such a fan-atical Heinlein fan, I'd been on the lookout for a method to meet the man as long as I can remember, and about April of 1973 I had a plan. *Publisher's Weekly* had run an ad announcing the release of Heinlein's new novel, *Time Enough For Love*, for June 19th and I figured I'd write a really super review for the *New York Times Book Review*, tying up its theme of long life with Jerome Tuccille's *Here Comes Immortality*, a recently-released book with strong, libertarian overtones. Aside from killing two birds with one stone, I thought this just might get me a nice letter from Mr. Heinlein which , through my diabolic intelligence and *bon vivant* personality, I could eventually turn into a invitation to meet him. The method was one used successfully by Sharon Presley and, Mr. Heinlein has since told me, first advocated by Benjamin Franklin: find out what the person you want to meet wants...and give it to him. (A variation of this technique is demonstrated in "We Also Walk Dogs." Note Dr. O'Neil and the Flower of Forgetfulness.)

I sent off to John Leonard, the *Times Book Review* editor, and several days later one of his assistants called me to come down to their offices—and pick up bound galleys of *Time Enough For Love*! I'd done it!

Well, at least I *thought* I had.

I was assigned 900 words for the two books—an impossibly short length, if you've ever tried it—and got in what I considered a pretty fair piece a week before the deadline. Then I sat back waiting for the review to be in. A month or so later I received a check for $100...but the review still wasn't scheduled, and since I'd been told minimum payment would be $125, I called up to find out what was going on. That's when I found out that "due to space limitations in the *Book Review*," mine wasn't going to be printed.

Rats. Other unprintables.

(John Leonard has since written his own review of

Time Enough For Love for the daily *Times* book page, and had Theodore Sturgeon review it in the *Book Review*. So much for that.)

I was, however, being allowed to submit my review elsewhere. Well, that wasn't so bad; I might even get paid twice for the same review. Hey, that wasn't bad *at all*.

I submitted it around to different magazines and newspapers, improving it and doubling the length in the course of rewriting, until I finally hit George Nobbe, editor of the New York *Sunday News*. He liked the idea of the review, but only had enough space for 600 words. So I typed up and sent him the Heinlein review alone, and a few days later he told me it was sold; it would be appearing in the next Sunday's edition.

The Thursday before he called me to say all bets were off.

It was now "high editorial policy" that only staff-written book reviews could be used. Rats. (Other unprintables.) He wanted to know, however, if I wanted to do an interview with Heinlein. Did I want to...? Is the bear Catholic? Does a Pope...well, you get the idea. "Fine," said George Nobbe. Did I know how to contact Heinlein? Sho'nuff!

So in a scenario right out of *Superman*, I contacted Clark Ken...er, that is, I called Sharon Presley at Laissez Faire Books. She put through a call to Mr. Heinlein relaying the *News* offer. And the next day, Thursday, June 26th, 4:14 p.m., E.D.T. (approx.) I picked up the telephone and The Voice said...and you already know what The Voice said.

(Talk about adequate preparation for a statistical universe! [See *Have Space Suit—Will Travel*.])

After I managed to stutter that I was me, Mr. Heinlein asked me what the project was all about. I told him, then he asked if I had time to chat a while. Did I have...? Is the Bear...aw, forget it. So to start off, he asked me what I wanted to ask. I said, "How do you know what you know?" I couldn't be sure with long distance, but I think he gasped. Thereafter we talked philosophy and just about everything else under the sun, then Mr. Heinlein said he wanted to know something about me. *Me.* I told him my entire life from birth. I told him about my father's career as a violinist. (Mr. Heinlein asked me to go slow enough to write it all down. A Farleyfile, perhaps? [See *Double Star*.])

We then talked about *his* life some more, and he asked me to send him a list of questions in advance of our taping the interview itself. Then we said goodbye. I exhaled about a minute later and noted the time: we'd talked just under two hours.

(Irrelevant interjection: That evening I went out with Sam Konkin & company to see the movie *Live and Let Die* and I guess I *was* pretty much walking on air. I mentioned that near the end of The Conversation I'd mentioned to Mr. Heinlein how much I'd admired his work since childhood and he'd replied that hero worship wasn't always the best thing for the hero. "Hero worship, hmmmph!" Sam commented. "Worship!—'Here, have my first begotten son!'")

I spent the next hour or so organizing my notes and the following is a partial list:

Heinlein Debriefing

1) Heinlein's answer to my first question was that he starts with the evidence of his five senses and postulates a real world because it makes it easier to take subways and such, as he occasionally must.

8) Heinlein calls himself an individualist, and remarked, "Ayn Rand is a bloody socialist compared to me." I think he was joking; we both laughed.

11) But no matter how much you feel like an individual, Heinlein says, you are but a link in the tree of human evolution. I asked if he thought survival of the species should be raised to the level of eschatology, and he replied that he eschewed the term (my phrasing) and prefers to use words of Anglo-Saxon origin. If I meant "of final importance," then yes; though not of *only* importance.

18) "I have never plotted any story I've ever written," said Heinlein. He continues that "plot" is something English professors talk about because they can't explain what it is writers *really* do.

The next day, Friday, I sent off three pages of questions to him special delivery and fidgeted all weekend. Monday, at about 3:35 p.m., E.D.T., by prearrangement, I went into George Nobbe's empty office at the *News* (he had taken the day off) with a cassette recorder and telephone pickup and put through The Call.

Mr. Heinlein answered and told me he'd just received my questions and hadn't had a chance to look them over yet. I said I was sure they would've been delivered the day before. "Yesterday was Sunday," Heinlein said. "I sent it special delivery," I said. He then told me he lived way out in the country (about a half hour outside Santa Cruz, Calif.) and there *wasn't* any special delivery there. Though he laughed and said he wouldn't expect a "city boy" to know that. I hadn't.

I went out and had a sandwich then called back in forty-five minutes. I started the tape and we talked for 3 1/2 hours, stopping only at hourly intervals to turn the cassettes. At the end, I asked if leftover material could be used for *New Libertarian Notes*. He said yes.

Who *is* Robert Anson Heinlein?

He was born in Butler, Missouri on July 7, 1907 into a large family tracing its roots back to a Bavarian-German ancestor who emigrated to America in 1756. Heinlein was raised in Kansas City, Mo., won an appointment to Annapolis where he was noted as a champion swordsman, and served on active duty as a line officer on destroyers and aircraft carriers until being disabled out of the Navy. He started writing science fiction in 1939 "to pay off a mortgage" and within two years was regarded as one of the leaders in the field.

Robert Heinlein has twice been Guest of Honor at the World Science Fiction Convention (1941 & 1961) and four of his novels (Double Star, *Starship Troopers*, *Stranger in a Strange Land*, and *The Moon is a Harsh*

Mistress) have won the Hugo Award given by the Convention's popular vote—an unmatched record. At a seminar on Heinlein I conducted at this past Worldcon in Toronto, the consensus of opinion in an off-the-cuff poll I took gave *Time Enough For Love* a good chance for a fifth.

Talking with Robert Heinlein is talking with the Platonic archetype of all his best characters. Heinlein is a fiery intellectual who feels as much at home with an anecdote as a syllogism. From the deference I paid him whenever we talked, Mr. Heinlein might have gotten the impression that I'm normally meek and timid. I'm not, Mr. Heinlein—really. Ask Sharon Presley; she'll set you straight.

The following will be the first installment of what is, in my biased opinion, the most interesting and comprehensive in-depth interview ever printed about Heinlein.

If I may be immodest to bring it up (and I have never been noted for my modesty), my story for the New York *Sunday News*, "Looking Upward Through The Microscope: Robert A. Heinlein," has been called by both Mr. and Mrs. Heinlein the best article, in style, content, and accuracy, of the many, many written about him over the years.

Any editors listening? Any of you want to buy a slightly worn book review?

*Footnote for the Pulpless.Com™ edition: Yes, this is the same Louis Rossetto who is founder and publisher of *Wired* Magazine!

The
Robert Heinlein
Interview

Conducted by J. Neil Schulman
June 30, 1973

Note for the Pulpless.Com™ edition: This interview appears *exactly* as it was edited by Robert A. Heinlein in 1973, with no deletions, additions, or changes.   —JNS, 1996

Schulman: All right. Why don't we start with question number one?

Heinlein: Question number one: "Do you believe time travel is possible or is it merely a fictional device?"

There is no basis for belief or non-belief in this question, Neil. We don't have any data from which to work. There is at present no satisfactory theory of time. We haven't the slightest idea of how you might get your teeth into the fabric of time—whatever it is. Time travel, *as of now*, comes under the head of fantasy, inasmuch as it requires one to postulate something about which we know nothing. I *do not* regard time travel as either impossible or possible. I have no opinion about its possibility or impossibility because we have no data on which to make a judgment. But it makes an excellent device for telling stories, particularly stories that speculate about the condition of mankind and his future, and so forth and so on; it's been used almost entirely for that purpose, including *A Connecticut Yankee In King Arthur's Court* which is very largely a social and political pamphlet expressed in story form, to go back to a time-travel story of the last century and one which doesn't even use a time machine—it just postulates it. And the same thing is true, of course, of H.G. Wells' *Time Machine* and his *When The Sleeper Wakes*. In both cases he was using a time-travel device in order to permit him to speculate about the human condition.

Schulman: If you *did* manage to find a time machine, would you go back and try strangling yourself as an infant to see if the universe would collapse around you?

Heinlein: No I wouldn't try it. [laughter] In the first place, I am not at all unhappy about having lived the life I've lived. In the second place, if I strangled the infant and the universe collapsed around me thereby— the solipsist's point of view—then I would have proved my point by *failing* to prove my point. I mean you wind up with a zero—with no *observer*, follow me? You wouldn't know if it worked or *not*. If you're going to engage in the notion that the universe ceases to exist if you die, then you're not entitled to an observer *outside* that to see what happens. Solipsism has its own logical paradoxes.

Schulman: Okay. We might as well proceed to question number two, then.

Heinlein: "I'd like to know more about your theory that 'no matter how individualistic you feel, you are really only part of an evolutionary organism.'"

Schulman: Did I quote you correctly on that?

Heinlein: You've placed a little emphasis in there: "really *only* a part of." What I believe I said—the book is across the room and I'm not going to dig it out—was that "you *are* part of an evolutionary organism" not "really *only* a part of." Difference in emphasis, do you follow me?

Schulman: Yes.

Heinlein: Just as you are J. Neil Schulman and you are also part of the population of an area known as New York City. But it isn't a case of J. Neil Schulman being "really *only* a part of" New York City. You *are* J. Neil Schulman and you also happen to be one of that population group called by that name. Now, *there is* a matter of emphasis here. You say, "Can you prove this?" Well, I can't prove that you are "really *only* a part of" but I observe that you *are* only a part of. No emphasis on it, we simply observe it. You have parents. You have at least the potentiality of offspring. I assume that you go along more or less at least with evolutionary theory.

Schulman: To a certain extent.

Heinlein: ...Yes. We simply observe that we are part of this continuing process.

Schulman: Now, I think what I was asking here was the more philosophical question...in other words, I can see that I have parents and come from an evolutionary chain.

Heinlein: Yes.

Schulman: But the phrase "evolutionary organism" seems to suggest that you have one being with central control or something...or at least some central *plan*.

Heinlein: It doesn't... I don't mean to imply that. Evolutionists differ in their notions as to whether or not there is any central plan or whether the whole matter is automatic, or what it may be. All I really meant is that although we feel as if we were discrete individuals, if you consider it in terms of four dimensions with time as the fourth dimension, you are part of a branch...a branching deal, with an actual physical connection going back into the past and physical connection extending into the future until such a time as it's chopped off. If you have no children then it's chopped off at that point. I have no children myself, however I'm not dead yet, either. I think, however, you are more interested in a later part here: "if so but we retain free will, why should we place the welfare of the whole organism above ourselves?" The question as to whether or not you place the welfare of your species—your race— above yourself is a matter for you to settle with yourself and for me to settle with me.

Schulman: On what basis?

Heinlein: [Quoting question] "If you say it's something you can't justify on a purely rational basis, then what other basis is there to justify it?" That's what you're getting at; you're trying to make it as either/or here between rational and irrational.

Schulman: Well…rational and *non*rational in any case.

Heinlein: All right. [Long pause] Uh, I'm trying to phrase this clearly. And you say this last question leads up to this next one: "Is there ever any justification to accept something on faith? How can you prove this since by doing so you are inherently rejecting reason as final arbiter?" Now, there are a lot of implications in your question, a lot of hidden assumptions in your question.

Schulman: I suppose so.

Heinlein: Yes, indeed. All the way through this I can see that you regard yourself as a rationalist and you regard reason as the final arbiter on anything.

Schulman: Well, I'm basically starting out with Ayn Rand's Objectivist epistemology.

Heinlein: Well, I'm not going to comment on Miss Rand's epistemology; I have notions of my own. Have you read anything by Alfred Korzybski?

Schulman: No, I'm familiar with his work only through your own; you've mentioned him quite a few times.

Heinlein: Only through my own. You haven't read *Science and Sanity*, for example?

Schulman: No, I haven't.

Heinlein: And you're not familiar with his epistemological approach?

Schulman: Only what you yourself have mentioned.

Heinlein: Uh, huh. [interruption] Uh, I've just been talking to Mrs. Heinlein; now let me see.

Let me invert these questions a bit. If you've read *Stranger in a Strange Land*, you've probably gathered what I think of faith. I do not regard faith as a basis on which to believe or disbelieve *anything*. On the other hand, Neil, there are many things—practically all of the important questions of philosophy—are not subject to final answers purely by reason. In my opinion, they are *not* subject to final answers simply by reason. This has been gone into a considerable extent by philosophers in the past, and there's even a term—a technical term—

for that called "noumena" as opposed to "phenomena." Phenomena are things that you can grasp through your physical senses or through measurements made with your physical senses through instruments and so forth and so on; in other words, phenomena are things that we can know about the physical universe. Noumena translates as the *un*knowable things. The unknowable things: What is the purpose of the universe? Why are you here on this earth? What should a man do with his life? All of those wide open, generalized, unlimited "whys." There are all noumena, and consequently they are not subject—consequently *by definition*—these things are not subject to final answers simply by reason. My own attitude on that is shown a bit in several places in this last book [*Time Enough For Love*] in which Lazarus Long indicates that he hasn't been able to find any purpose to the universe any more significant than gametes using zygotes to create more gametes. He expresses it that way in one place, then he turns it over, turns it upside down, and expresses it another way to the effect that as far as he knows, there's no more important purpose to the universe than making a baby with the help of a woman you love. And yet obviously neither of these things are answers; they are just expressions of what Lazarus Long happens to like. Now, do you happen to like chocolate malted milks?

Schulman: Uh, yes.

Heinlein: Now, do you like them better than *strawberry* malted milks?

Schulman: Yeah, I would say so.

Heinlein: Can you justify that by reason?

Schulman: No, I would say that it's a purely subjective judgment.

Heinlein: That's right. That is correct. It doesn't involve faith and it doesn't involve reason.

Schulman: But I'm using internal data; there *is* data which I am acting upon.

Heinlein: That's right. The internal data tells you that you like it better...but it doesn't tell you *why*. This applies also to a great many things about the universe: it's your own internal, subjective evaluation of it, not any final answers given by reason or rationality.

Schulman: This brings up the end of *Methuselah's Children* in which Lazarus Long seems to be taking just about the opposite attitude.
    I have a quote here:
    "'The last two and a half centuries have just been my adolescence...men...never had enough time to tackle the important questions. Lots of capacity and not enough time to use it properly.'"

And then he's asked: "'How do you propose to tackle the important questions?'

"'How should I know? Ask me again in about five hundred years.'

"'You think that will make a difference?'

"'I do. Anyhow it'll give me time to poke around and pick up some interesting facts...'"

A little later: "'...Maybe there aren't any reasons.'

"'Yes, maybe it's just one colossal big joke with no point to it.' Lazarus stood up and scratched his ribs. 'But I can tell you this...here`s one monkey who's going to keep on climbing, and looking around him to see what he can see, as long as the tree holds out.'"

Heinlein: And that's exactly what he's doing at the end of the next book.

Schulman: Just holding on.

Heinlein: Uh, yes. In the mean time it is postulated that he's had a couple of thousand years trying this, that, and the other thing, and he has reached *one* point. He has reached *one* opinion; it's stated flatly in the early part of the book: that you cannot get final answers about the universe from *inside*. He said you'd have to get outside and take a look at it. And the man he's talking to, Weatheral, says: "Then you believe in immortality?" [In the book, the word "afterlife" is used.] And Lazarus says, "Wait, wait, wait, wait, now—hold everything! I didn't say I believed in immortality; I don't *believe* in anything. Because belief gets in the way of *facts.*" He's made certain observations and they've given him certain limited opinions, and among the limited opinions he has is the one working hypothesis that there *are no* final answers to be obtained from a human being inside the universe, that the position of observation doesn't permit that—to get any final answers. Follow me?

Schulman: Okay.

Heinlein: There's nothing inconsistent about the end of *Methuselah's Children* and what the man has to say a couple of thousand years later; it's just that he's had a couple of thousand years *trying* this that he said he was going to try and he still hasn't gotten any *final* answers.

Schulman: I suppose this leads up to question number fifteen on page two.

Heinlein: Question fifteen on page two: "What would a 2,300 year old man know that we don't?" Neil, I haven't the slightest idea; I'm not even a hundred, yet! Remember, this thing's a work of *fiction.* "Wouldn't it take a 2,300 year old man to *write* the memoirs of Lazarus Long?" Of course it would, but do you know any? This is a work of fiction. If I've managed to make him at all convincing as an extremely old man—not necessarily twenty-three centuries but extremely old—then it's successful as a work of art, as a work of fiction. If it entertains the reader in the course of doing that then it's a *commercially* successful work of art. But I am not twenty-three hundred years old; I'm not even a century, yet.

Schulman: I just wanted to check that out.

Heinlein: All right. [Reading next part of question] "How did Shaw's *Back to Methuselah* influence this if at all?"

I read Shaw's *Back to Methuselah* about ten years before I started writing—oh, sometime in the thirties. I haven't looked at it since, don't remember it too clearly. I've read most of Shaw's plays and some of his essays and I suppose I've been influenced by him, just as I've been influenced by everything I've ever read, seen, tasted, felt, so forth and so on. But as for specific influence of one book on the other, they're rather different. As I recall, in the latter part of *Back to Methuselah* everyone has gotten extremely cautious because they're afraid they might die. They've got so much to lose. Lazarus Long never suffers from that although I do indicate that some of the other Methuselahs or Howard people do have a bit of that trouble. But, I don't remember it too well; after all, I didn't see the play: I read it *once* something over forty years ago—or just about forty years ago—and I've never reread it since.

Schulman: I think what I was referring to was a specific line that Richard Friedman, our *NLN* review editor [when this was taped], pointed out to me—something along the line that it would take long life to plan anything, that we simply don't have enough time to decide what the questions are to ask.

Heinlein: Oh, yes; I agree with that, and this also makes it difficult for me to pretend to be a twenty-three century old man because, as I pointed out to you, I'm not even a century yet. I've noticed that you've paid quite a bit of attention to *Have Space Suit—Will Travel.* Do you recall in there, I think it's the Mother Thing appealing on behalf of the human race: "But my lord peers, they are all so very *young*." She's asking a certain amount of forbearance for the human race because it's so young. And that's about the situation we're in: our civilization is very young. None of us live long enough to cope with too much. About the time we begin to get our thoughts straightened out we begin to go senile. Or, in the mean time, we've been knocked over by a taxicab or died of the plague or something else. We *don't* live that long.

Shall we finish the rest of that same question?

Schulman: Okay.

Heinlein: "Do you have any comments on the Wandering Jew legends which you've made reference to in several of your books?"

I don't recall the other references I've made to it but throughout my books I refer constantly to mythological matters, biblical matters, so forth and so on. Call these cultural ties, if you like. It comes under the head of putting a little flavor in the stew, that's all. The Wandering Jew legend, I really don't know anything about it. The *Encyclopedia Britannica* doesn't have much to say about it. It's apocryphal; there have been some good stories from it. General Lew Wallace's *The Prince of India*—which isn't nearly as well known as his book *Ben Hur* from which this movie was made—was based on the Wandering Jew legend and there have been several others. It's a nice, romantic legend that has considerable story value to it. You might say that I grabbed it and renamed him Lazarus Long and made this book out of it.

Schulman: That's one of the first things I was thinking—that you might've been intending Lazarus Long to be the Wandering Jew—until he made reference to having met him.

Heinlein: As I recall—I seem to recall writing that paragraph—I don't think I specifically used it— Sometimes one does put something like that into a story in order the deny an assumption of that sort? I don't think I put it in for that purpose; I think it was just Lazarus Long enjoying one of his *whoppers* again. Lying in his teeth! [laughter]

Schulman: Is there anything in the book he *believed*?

Heinlein: Oh, sure. If you examine the fashion in which

it is written, the story of the adopted daughter is written cold sober all the way through.

Schulman: That was, if I remember, third person?

Heinlein: No, it's both third person and first person, because part of it is narration recounting the events that take place on New Beginnings and part of it he's talking to the computer, Minerva. But he's being dead serious all the way through. But when he's simply engaged in conversation with other people... Mark Twain once said, "First research the facts. Then distort them to prove your case." [laughter] This character is sort of a Mark Twain character. I even have him come from Mark Twain's general part of the country. The Ozarks are noted for their whoppers.

Schulman: Okay. What about the story of David Lamb?

Heinlein: David Lamb? What about him?

Schulman: Well, is it based on anybody you know or material you drew from your own Annapolis experience or...?

Heinlein: You trying to get me sued? [laughter] This is why authors put disclaimers on the front of books.

Schulman: Which is the biggest lie in any book.

Heinlein: Oh, sure. That character is fictional, but it is of course based on various things I knew, experienced, people I've known, when I was in the Navy. And obviously in telling the story Lazarus Long is having fun with it and not necessarily sticking closely to the truth. In fact, even in a casual reading of it, you can see big holes in it—where things don't fit, where the chronology is wrong—where the locations are wrong—all sorts of things.

Schulman: I've only read it three times; I haven't had a chance to analyze it yet.

Heinlein: Well, for example, just casually on the side he locates the Naval Academy at West Point.

Schulman: I'd thought that was just a failing of memory.

Heinlein: Probably. Possibly. Maybe. In any case, there are things like that through the story; it's not told *at all* in the dead serious way in which "The Tale of the Adopted Daughter" is told. Entirely different sort of story. It's partially a piece of satire. This man, no matter what he did, took the easiest way out, the laziest way out—and it always worked.

Schulman: I can empathize with that.

Heinlein: [Laughing] Yes.

Schulman: Would you like to go back to question number four?

Heinlein: Sure. Let me turn the pages here; oh, here we are. [Softly;] There's too much on this desk; there's *always* too much on this desk.

"About the space program. I know you are extremely impressed by the accomplishments of NASA. (Well, so am I.)" The accomplishment of NASA that I'm most impressed by is how they manage to take the most romantic subject I know of and by careful application make it incredibly *dull*. [Laughter] I am not disparaging the engineering accomplishments nor the heroic accomplishments of astronauts in saying that. I'm talking primarily about their P.R.O.! [Returning to question] "But since it was financed with tax money"—and your parenthetical remark in there ["(which I believe is the same thing as stolen money)"—JNS]—"isn't the expenditure of any more money by government on space programs illegitimate?" Now the word "illegitimate" has a technical meaning, Neil: it means illegal. And the answer to that is that the expenditure is not illegal; it's perfectly legal—the laws are on the books. However, you used it in a philosophical sense. I *think* you used it equivalent to "immoral."

Schulman: Well, you see, I equate legality with being based on natural law, and I see that statutory law is a nullification of that. [I am here using the term natural law in its economic as well as metaphysical sense. For an economic analysis of government intervention, see Murray N. Rothbard's *Power and Market;* for a philosophical analysis see his *For A New Liberty.* — JNS, 1973]

Heinlein: Well, now natural law—the concept of natural law —is one that many philosophers have tried to put over, but as far as I'm concerned natural law are things like the second law of thermodynamics—that entropy always increases—which could be defined mathematically. Natural law are the facts that we know about the physical world.

Schulman: I believe that also in the "Notebooks [of Lazarus Long]" you have a statement that if you can't talk about it in math, it's not science, it's just opinion.

Heinlein: That is correct; if you can't talk about it *quantitatively* it is not science, it is just opinion. And on most of these matters of natural law, each philosopher that's attempted to do this has come up with a different set of natural laws from the one next door. Now, I don't know which philosopher you follow on this. Do I make myself clear?

Schulman: Yes.

Heinlein: I should say at this point that my stories have consistently shown space travel being undertaken by private enterprise. That I regard as a matter of taste—

my own taste. Which apparently agrees with yours.

Schulman: Right.

Heinlein: [Continuing question] "Shouldn't the entire program be turned over to private enterprise to try and make a profit?" I don't like the expression "turned over." Shouldn't the entire program be *sold* to private enterprise?

Schulman: Well, since from my anarchistic point of view I don't see that government can legitimately own property...

Heinlein: All right; how can they *legitimately* pass on a title to it by "turning it over" to private enterprise?

Schulman: I guess there's a philosophical contradiction in there...

Heinlein: Yes.

Schulman: But if you accept the presence of government as an unwanted, already existing thing, you're always backed into corners like that. [This problem is soluble only by postulating a post-revolutionary situation in which anarchocapitalist arbitration agencies are liquidating all government properties and returning them to those victims with valid claims.]

Heinlein: Well, in any case…"For example, my colleague at *New Libertarian Notes*, Sam Konkin, says that if he were running the space program he'd simply pay back his investment by running shiploads of moon rocks back to earth to sell as ornaments and jewelry." Well, I wonder if Mr. Konkin has considered the economic law of diminishing returns at that point?

Schulman: I think he did take that into account; he had several other schemes like that…The point he was trying to make was that if somebody like him could figure out a way to bring back profits, sooner of later some sort of trade would be built out of this.

Heinlein: Oh, yes. I am quite certain that space travel is going to be enormously profitable in the long run. But that particular stunt…By the way, that is included in this enterprise of the Hubbards; I suppose you've heard about that?

Schulman: L. Ron Hubbard?

Heinlein: No, no no. *Colonel* Hubbard, and his wife. Let me see. I'd like to find one of their magazines around here; I don't see one offhand and haven't time to look. In any case, they are trying to get together an organization to buy one of the remaining Apollos—to *buy from the government* one of the remaining Apollos— and start in on a *commercial* venture to get the human race out into the solar system and on out. They think it could be done by private enterprise and they're trying to do it. In other words, they have a point of view that is consonant with yours and consonant with mine.

Schulman: We might as well bring in question number ten here, because it's related to number five.

Heinlein: All right; let me get to it. Number ten: "This question is related to number five. Have you heard the claims made by Dr. Andrew J. Galambos several years before the space program started that he could put a man on the moon for $100,000? If so, do you have any comments?" Who is Galambos?

Schulman: Galambos is a Californian; he's at the Free Enterprise Institute which is in the Los Angeles area.

Heinlein: And what is the doctorate in—do you know?

Schulman: I think it's in economics. [I was incorrect: Galambos's degree is in astrophysics.]

Heinlein: How far back did he make this remark?

Schulman: Oh! I can't give anywhere near an exact date; I think it was as far back as the fifties that he was claiming that he had a plan to finance it.

Heinlein: Yes. Well, the fifties. I have to consider inflation as to what a hundred thousand dollars meant then and what a hundred thousand means now. Well, let's put it a few years back and figure that he'd be talking about a considerably more than a hundred thousand now; but if it's anything like that recent it wouldn't have more than doubled—the amount he's talking about—in buying power.

Now. I happen to be a quite experienced R and D engineer myself—not in space activities but in aircraft and in high altitudes work, things like that. Also, I built this house from which I'm talking to you right now—built it fairly recently. I spent considerably more than a hundred thousand dollars on it. I know *durn well* that I couldn't *begin* to build a spaceship—completely shut of all the difficulties of working through the government or anything like that; I mean if I simply had the cash and undertook to build it myself—I couldn't begin to build it for anything like a hundred thousand dollars. I do not think that Dr. Galambos is an experienced engineer of *any* sort.

Schulman: I think the point he was trying to make is that if the government had allowed private research to be pursued in this instead of every time something was discovered clamping a top security on it that—

Heinlein: The government *did not* do that. On the contrary, everything that NASA puts is *open*.

Schulman: *Everything?*

Heinlein: Everything. And they also put out a thing saying; now what subjects are you interested in? As a result of that, having noted several of the subjects that I was interested in, I have received so many, many pounds—so many millions of words—of research reports, that I finally had to move them up into my storehouse because I no longer had library space for them. Everything that NASA puts out, they do not have anything classified. *Nothing.* Now, let me distinguish between anything that the Air Force might be doing. The two activities are conducted separately: the Air Force does have classified espionage satellites, for example. But NASA does not, and they don't work the same places, they don't work together. Everything that NASA does—from the start by law—was to be open and unclassified and it *has* been. This is one of the things that I have cited—and that Arthur Clarke has cited—as being a payoff on the space program right now. Expensively as they've done it, nevertheless all that bread cast on the waters has already come back severalfold in the way of unclassified new technology that doesn't even have patents on it. You can get these things and you can use them all you please. I know that a lot of people are not aware of this but anyone in engineering that has any engineering interest is likely to be aware of it if he has taken the trouble to have himself placed on the mailing list.

Schulman: Well, I guess that was just a mistake on *my* part. [Even more ironic is that Galambos is the father of the theory of primary property that states that *all* ideas are private property and should be copyrighted.]

Heinlein: Yes. However, the thing that makes it so expensive when you do things through government is the *enormous* amount of bureaucracy and red tape. This is not alone, however, characteristic of government; it is characteristic of almost any big human organization. You get one of those really big corporations and you have a tremendous bureaucratic structure inside the corporation itself.

Schulman: However, I've heard that because of competition demands, if you take the bureaucracy of a private corporation, it's maybe around *ten percent* of that which government manages to generate.

Heinlein: Well, I've seen a bit of both and I *don't* think the increase in efficiency on the part of free enterprise is that great. The justification for free enterprise is not that it's more efficient, *but that it's free*! Follow me?

Schulman: Yes.

Heinlein: This reminds me of a story—oh, it's from a preface to a book about some civil liberties cases about forty years back; I wish I could remember the author; he was a prominent civil liberties lawyer. But he told this anecdote about down South, some time postbellum, but probably fifty or sixty or seventy years back, in which this Southern gentleman was attempting to explain to the Yankee friend that the Negro had actually been better off under slavery. He says, "I'll prove it to you." He says, "Oh, Tom, Uncle; come over here." And this old Negro shuffled over. And he said to him, "Uncle, you were a slave, weren't you?"

"Yes, Cap'n."

"Tell me. Do you *eat* as well now as you did when you were a slave?"

"Oh, no, Cap'n. Sometimes pickin's might poor."

"Do you work as hard as you did when you were a slave?"

"Oh, no. I works *lots* harder *now*."

"Do you live in as good a house?"

"That little shack I'm in now, the rain comes in all the time."

He says, "Then you were better off when you were a slave, weren't you?"

And the old Negro *didn't* agree, he *didn't* say yes; he scratched his head and he said slowly, "Boss, there's somethin' about this heah freedom that I lahkes!"

Schulman: [Laughing] Okay.

Heinlein: In other words, you don't have to justify private enterprise on the basis of its being more efficient than government—although it *usually* is. Not always, but usually.

Schulman: Well, at least it keeps the bureaucracies

running against each other so you have a bit of a choice.

Heinlein: Yes, and that's even possible inside the government—I'll tell you about a case in a moment. The justification for free enterprise is that it's *free*. "Sort of a looseness about this heah freedom that I lahkes!" That's all.

Schulman: Okay. I don't need any further justification, myself, either.

Heinlein: It's a matter of taste. It's the way you feel about it, It's the way I feel about it. You don't have to prove it.

Schulman: Okay.

Heinlein: Oh. Competition. I thought and still think that one of the mistakes that they made in this government was when they converted the Army and Navy into the Department of Defense and created the Air Force Department and simply incorporated it therein. You know what it did? It removed from a government system one of the few examples of healthy competition we see in government. The thing that kept the Navy on its toes was the Army, and the thing that kept the Army on its toes was the Navy, and the point at which they had to fight was right over the appropriations. And they weren't able—either one of them—to judge it for themselves: it was up to the Congress. And they had to *compete*. Now, all through the military service there are attempts to set up competition—oh, between ships, between companies, between squads, so forth and so on—because there are a hell of a lot of military officers—most of them perhaps—who realize that the competition which any socialistic set-up inherently lacks—and the Army and Navy *are* socialistic set-ups—is a shortcoming. It makes it less efficient. So they set up these artificial competitions just to keep them on their toes. There are plenty—Perhaps most professional military men are *acutely* aware that the Army and the Navy do not have it unless they deliberately build it up as a sort of a game.

Schulman: I guess I could bring up the point in question number eleven on page two at this point.

Heinlein: All right. "In the 'Notebooks of Lazarus Long' there is a statement that since anarchists and pacifists refuse to support a state, they deserve no protection from that state. Wouldn't you say—at least about anarchists—that this statement is irrelevant because anarchists don't even *want* protection 'from' the state, they want protection *against* it?" Now. Neil. You have in there an assumption contrary to fact. And that is that there is such a thing as anarchists which agree on any one thing. [Laughter] There are as many sorts of anarchism as there are anarchists and you sure as hell know it by now!

Schulman: [Laughing] Yes.

Heinlein: You've been in it a relatively short time—I mean by my time scale, not by Lazarus Long's—but you've certainly seen it. How do anarchists spend their time? Why, they spend it fighting with *other* anarchists. Isn't that true?

Schulman: [Still laughing] Well, a few of us manage to get along.

Heinlein: Well, you sent me first this *New Libertarian Notes* and I noticed that the lead article in there was one panning the hell out of the magazine called *Reason*. [Laughter] And blasting these *revisionists, dissidents*, and so forth. There are as many sorts of anarchists as there are anarchists.

Schulman: Okay.

Heinlein: Incidentally, I'm delighted to have both magazines in the house as I frequently find something in each of them that disagrees with my own point of view. It does me no good to read something that *agrees* with my own point of view. I want to read something that disagrees with my own point of view, follow me?

Schulman: Okay.

Heinlein: You can't learn from a man who agrees with

you. But the point I wanted to bring out was that there are one hell of a lot of anarchists who think that there is pie in the sky and that Santa Claus sill lives and that somehow, some way, policemen will still be on the corner no matter if they do away with them. There are an awful lot of starry-eyed ignoramuses among anarchists, Neil—just as there are in any *other* political point of view. And there are plenty of them who *still* expect the government to protect them, and they really don't have imagination enough to visualize a completely lawless situation.

[Therein lies the value of libertarian science fiction—JNS, 1973]

Schulman: In a recent book by Harry Browne called *How I Found Freedom In An Unfree World*—I don't know if you're familiar with it or not...

Heinlein: I've seen some reviews. I haven't read it. I've seen some reviews and things of it.

Schulman: Well one of the things he brings out in there is the basic anarchocapitalist viewpoint—which he's bringing to the bestselling reading public for the first time—in which he's saying, "Well, suppose you didn't *have* police anymore—what would you do?" And he says, "Well, you'd probably lock your doors and stay out of unsafe neighborhoods and keep your children away from unsavory people—isn't that exactly what you're doing *now*?"

Heinlein: Yes.

Schulman: And then he goes on to state the basic difference *we* have with government: that it provides relatively very little protection *at all*; if it does anything it simply provides a little retaliation to act as a deterrent—and it doesn't even do very much of *that*.

Heinlein: Well, we could get into a long discussion here of political and anarchist theory; all that I was getting at is that there are many anarchists who don't really get their teeth into that notion that there *could* be anything to be afraid of in an utterly lawless community. Now it is very much to the point to realize that the community is *already* quite lawless, as Harry Browne points out there. I'm one of those self-help people myself. Cop on the corner? I said I was fifteen miles out in the country; I'm fifteen miles from the nearest police service of any sort. It would take over half an hour for a sheriff's car to get here if he started right now. I mean if he were available and started right now. In other words we have no police protection. And, as you may have heard, Santa Cruz is noted as the murder capital of the world; it's a small town and we've had nineteen murders so far this year. Just a second. [pause] I had to shift position; my old bones were getting tired. Well, I believe in self-help. I'm quite a good shot. In fact I used to teach it. And my place is surrounded with a seven-foot-high steel fence topped with barbed wire and controlled by an electric gate....There are a number of people who can't seem to realize that things could be mighty rough—even rougher than they are *now*—if there wasn't the slightest bit of deterrence. I believe in deterrence, myself. I know quite well that there are a number of people walking the streets today alive and well only because there's a law with a certain *implied* punishment—even if it doesn't take place too often—for killing somebody. I'm not talking about anyone in particular either as the object or as the subject; I just say that I *know* that there are many times when somebody would *durn well* get killed if somebody else didn't feel that it was a *little* bit dangerous to go killing somebody. You might get arrested; you might get thrown in the hoosegow, and at least it would cause you dreadful inconvenience even if they didn't hang you.

Schulman: Well, of course, I can agree with the idea of deterrence to a great extent, but I disagree with your premise that you need government to provide the deterrent. Of course my own view is based on the theories of Murray Rothbard and several other people here in the movement, about private protection agencies, and private armies, and settling disputes through private arbitration. Competing agencies.

Heinlein: Yes, I've read a good deal of this. I don't think that we can manage to settle matters of detail about political philosophy on the time and toll charges of the

Daily News. So many things have been opened up at this point that you know quite well that it could go on for days and days and days and many thousands of words. I'm inclined to evaluate those things about private protection agencies and how protection could simply be left to the marketplace about equal to Karl Marx's notion that after the perfected socialism the state would wither away. You remember that was one of the predictions, that socialism led to anarchism through the state withering away. That was the happy condition of the future under Marx's predictions. Well, Marx turned out to be mistaken, at least so far as any evidence of the state withering away is concerned in the numerous countries that call themselves communist.

Schulman: Well, I certainly don't think you had to run a trial run on it to find out; I think it was pretty evident from the inconsistencies in what he was saying.

Heinlein: Yes. And, no doubt, you have read a number of things criticizing this notion of leaving protection entirely to the marketplace, too. I would be delighted to see a circumstance under which we needed no laws, no protection, so forth and so on. None of the philosophers that I have encountered have been able to convince me that this is practical in the real world, that it could be done. It is much more likely that if we had, for a short time, a condition of anarchy, that shortly after there we would have a condition of fascism that would grow up from a sort of vigilantism until finally a man on a horseback was in charge.

Schulman: Well, you see there's where—of course you're right; we don't have enough time to really get into this.

Heinlein: Yes.

Schulman: The only question I'd want to ask is have you read, for instance, *The Market For Liberty* by the Tannehills, or *Precondition For Peace And Prosperity: Rational Anarchy* by Richard and Ernestine Perkins, or *For A New Liberty* by Dr. Rothbard? All three go into the theories in quite a bit of detail.

Heinlein: I have read a number of these things—not necessarily ones that you've mentioned—but I've been reading on this subject for considerably more than the past forty years. And no one of them has convinced me yet. What we *do* have on this globe in respect to nations is a condition of anarchy between nations, despite something that we laughingly call international law.

Schulman: This is a point Dr. Rothbard makes frequently. He says we already have international anarchy; why not just decentralize down to the individual level?

Heinlein: Because along comes the bully boys. And if the bully boys band together then the people who simply want to be left alone have to band together.

Schulman: *Fine.* I'm not disagreeing with this.

Heinlein: Yes.

Schulman: However, to use Franz Oppenheimer's definitions I would much rather provide my protection through the economic means, rather than the political means.

Heinlein: Well, I think that we had better chop this off.

Schulman: Right.

Heinlein: Because it is too long; the *Daily News* can't *possibly* use it in depth. You've got twelve hundred words, something like that.

Schulman: Fifteen hundred, it turns out.

Heinlein: Fifteen hundred. You couldn't possible discuss the theory of anarchism in that space.

Schulman: Right. Well, hopefully, one of these days we'll be able to get it settled just between the two of us.

Heinlein: Well, I think we'll probably still be discussing it as long as both of us are alive. It isn't that I wouldn't like to *see* a condition of complete freedom;

you saw me describe that in Happy Valley. And you also saw Lazarus Long cope with the bully boys. But he nevertheless suggested that Happy Valley was pretty highly selective to start with for several reasons. And that as long as they had a low population they could get along simply with the Golden Rule. And they were beginning—he indicates that as things got a little more complicated—they started having a little more in the way of rules. But even at that he was sill talking about an agrarian society with a very low population. But let's move on to other matters out of fairness to the *Daily News*.

I would say that my position is not too far from that of Ayn Rand's; that I would like to see government reduced to no more than internal police and courts, external armed forces—with the other matters handled otherwise. I'm sick of the way the government sticks its nose into *every*thing, now.

Schulman: Okay. I think I'm going to have to turn over my tape right about now. Let's hold on for a second while I do so.

[AFTER THE TAPE IS TURNED]

Schulman: Okay. How about question number five? [A number of questions relating to the Nixon Administration, impeachment, and relations with communist countries]

Heinlein: Let's leave that one alone.

Schulman: Okay.

Heinlein: The reason I want to leave it alone is because like it or not the people you mentioned, at the present time, have tremendous responsibilities and I have no wish to jiggle their arms or second-guess them or be a Sunday-morning quarterback. It's *very* complicated and you don't have to like a man to know he's Officer of the Deck at the moment.

Schulman: Okay.

Heinlein: Number seven would be next, if you want that one.

Schulman: All right.

Heinlein: "Do you consider the revolution in *The Moon is a Harsh Mistress* to be a success?" I'm not sure what you mean by success; I described what happened and you can evaluate it to suit yourself. What happened in the long run appears in the *first* paragraph of the book and then again in the last paragraph. So far as Manny is concerned, the moon has acquired far too much government, they've thrown off the dictatorial rule from above and now they're getting far too much government from democratic means. It's not to his taste—nor to mine nor to yours. But I simply described what happened. I *might* say that there is implied there my own belief that government is an almost incurable disease of mankind when you get anything resembling a dense population.

Schulman: And I think you also make a point in *Time Enough For Love*—I think Lazarus makes the statement—that any time you get a large enough population you have absolutely no privacy any more and it's time to move on.

Heinlein: In fact he defines it as when the population reaches the point where they require I.D.'s. Now, let me comment on that in my own case.

When I was born the population of the United States was seventy-five million. Take a look at it now. When I first went in the service, you didn't even have to have a birth certificate. I didn't get a birth certificate until I was nearly fifty years old—a so-called "delayed" birth certificate. We didn't have I.D.'s—I mean to say a member of the military forces did not carry an I.D. on his person—back when I started in. He simply didn't; there *weren't* any. Very much smaller population, very much smaller organization, so forth and so on. And now we've reached the point where every time I turn around somebody asks me for my social security number; I had it forced on me. Any time a place gets densely enough populated for things like this to happen, it's time to move on. *I've* moved on to what extent I can; I live out in the country. I've taken a look at all the rest of this globe and I can say this for the United States; it's the worst possible country on the globe *except for all the others*. And as for California, California has *tremendous* shortcomings; it simply happens to be better than the rest for my taste. *For my taste*. Alaska has a very small population but it has a horrible climate and I'm tired of shoveling snow.

Schulman: My friend, Sam Konkin, is a bit of a Canadian chauvinist and he's always telling me about the glories of Alberta.

Heinlein: Oh, yes. He's perfectly right in that—if you're willing to put up with fifty degrees below zero; I'm *not*.

Schulman: Okay.

Heinlein: I've done the best I can under the circumstances to get as much freedom as I can by self-help methods.

Schulman: Okay. There's a second part to that question.

Heinlein: Okay.

Schulman: And even a third.

Heinlein: Oh, yes. "One of our group of libertarians, David Friedman, believes that Prof locked out Manny and Wyoh from further conversation with Mike, then committed suicide to prevent Mike from using his powers as a dictatorial tyrant." Well, inasmuch as Prof died right on stage, suicide seems sort of unlikely to me. You remember how he died? He was *speaking* at the moment.

Schulman: Right.

Heinlein: He's on a platform and speaking.

Schulman: Of course, I *could* think of several ways it could be done.

Heinlein: Oh, yes, surely. So far as the author of the story is concerned, I never had any such theory in mind. David Friedman is mistaken about that. So far as I could, that story—told in the first person—was told as accurately as Manny could tell it. Of course his viewpoint is limited.

Schulman: Okay.

Heinlein: "Is that what you intended? If not, what did you intend?" I intended to tell the story that the words set forth.

Schulman: Okay, that's self explanatory.

Heinlein: And as for the revolution being a success, success is a word—used with respect to a revolution or any attempt of that sort—that involves a subjective judgment. It's clear from *Manny's* standpoint that it is something *less* than a success. The final result—the final outcome—is not entirely to his taste. He's thinking about moving on to where things are looser.

Schulman: Okay. How about question number six, now?

Heinlein: "What would *Da Capo* have been like if you'd written it right after *Methuselah's Children?*" [*Da Capo* was the original title for *Time Enough For Love*— listed on the "Future History" chart—when Heinlein planned it back in the forties—JNS] Well in the first place I would have written it right after *Methuselah's Children.* So I'm reasonably certain that it would have been somewhat different from what it is, in fact *very* different. Look, I've lived more than a generation—in human terms—between those two books. It would be surprising if I hadn't changed some, grown some, changed my evaluations a bit in the course of that time, but in any case I did *not* write it then. And these *are* works of fiction.

Schulman: Okay.

Heinlein: All right. "Do you believe, as some of my friends have claimed, that you 'copped out' by resolving the matters of the Jockaira gods only in conversation?" Look, I'm not dead, yet. What makes your friends think that I won't write that story?

Schulman: They're hoping you will! In fact Sam Konkin—when I mentioned that I was still hoping you might write such a story—suggested that you should entitle it *Del Segno*, which means "from the sign."

Heinlein: Well, I used a musical analog all the way through this thing; it's Aria Da Capo and that's why the last part is "Da Capo." Aria Da Capo simply means to go back to the beginning...which he did.

Schulman: Yes, he certainly did.

I have to say that I disagree with one point that you made in our last conversation; that pornography is literature written to create an erection, and that you didn't think that this was the case with the last part of *Time Enough For Love.* I can name at least three friends who read through that last part *with* an erection.

Heinlein: [Laughing] How old were they?

Schulman: Right about my age.

Heinlein: Well, look—at the age of which you speak, almost everything makes you horny. The last part of that is certainly not pornography such as you can buy on Forty-Second Street. There *is* a great difference between realistic treatment of sex and pornographic treatment, and all I can say about that is that it was not *intended* to have that effect but if it did, my congratulations to you!

Schulman: Okay. How about the next part of number six? ["What really happened at the Families' meeting of 2012?"]

Heinlein: The Families' meeting of 2012? Nobody knows what happened at the Families' meeting of 2012 but Lazarus and he ain't talkin'! The point is, if you take timing on the thing, this is the point at which the Families had to make a decision as to how they were to deal with what they could see was an upcoming dictatorship. Just consider the date involved on the thing. That ties in with the story—oh, something "Empire…"

Schulman: "Logic of Empire"?

Heinlein: "Logic of Empire" and "If This Goes On—" and so forth. It was the date of a growing political crisis, and they're having to decide what they're going to do, and then there are indications later—in *Methuselah's Children* and elsewhere—that what they *did* do was go underground as thoroughly as they could, and distribute their wealth here and there under various and sundry dummies. Quite evidently Lazarus Long thought that their intentions were too mild—that they should do something far more dramatic—and 2,000 years later he is unwilling to argue the point as to whether his judgment was better or worse than of men long since dead. I don't particularly expect to do a story about the Families' meeting of 2012—all I have are some notes—and I'm not sure that it constitutes a story. Now. [Quoting from last part of question six] "I have to admit that my first thought when I started reading *Time Enough For Love* was shock and sadness to learn that Andy Libby had been dead over a thousand years." Well, if I write another story about Lazarus, it might turn out that Andy Libby *isn't* dead...at the time *that* story takes place.

Schulman: Oooh!

Heinlein: You see, my stories jump around in time, they always *have*. They are not written in the sequence in which they appear on the time-chart that John Campbell published a long time ago, not at all in that sequence.

Schulman: Speaking of the chart, there are two stories on there which are a bit of a mystery to quite a few of us; "Word Edgewise" and "Fire Down Below." [Two of the "Future History's" "unwritten" stories.]

Heinlein: I can indicate to you what each was about and they're—both of them—stories that I don't, at present, have plans for writing. I might; all I have are notes. But look, Neil—I probably don't have time to write too many more stories, and I have lots of other things I want to do besides writing stories. Like it or not I'm not going to last any twenty-three centuries. "Fire Down Below" concerned a revolution in Antarctica and "Word Edgewise" concerned Zebediah Scudder [sic] taking over the United States through his church.

Schulman: Wasn't that also "The Sound of His Wings"?

Heinlein: Well, there are two stories involved in there; both of them were intended to be novellas when I originally planned them many years ago. But I doubt if I will get around to writing these. I'd rather tackle something else. I have well over a hundred stories— with notes and outlines and so forth—in my files; most of them will never be written. I mean it's physically impossible simply for the reason that I acquire more stories each year than I write. I have more stories on file, unwritten, than I have written in my entire life-time, and my backlog gets larger each year. So it has to be a matter of choosing the story that I happen to want to write.

Schulman: Uh, huh.

Heinlein: And if I have that many stories left unwritten now, I will have *still more* stories left unwritten if I manage to last for a good many years longer, because it gets more so each year.

Schulman: I think I can understand that because I find myself writing maybe one story for every thirty story-ideas I get.

Heinlein: That's right. All right. [Quoting last part of question six:] "I had expected the book to start telling about his and Lazarus`s trips exploring for real estate." I had rather expected that, too, except that I had to pick and choose what I would put into this story; you can't cover twenty-three centuries in one book. Libby's and Lazarus Long's real estate adventures are not of the significance—I mean they're primarily adventures— they're not of the significance of the stuff that I *did* write, in my opinion. That book, despite its enormous bulk, is far more characterized by what I left out than by what I put in. [Chuckling] Twenty-three centuries.

Schulman: There's one thing that comes to mind that I didn't put on my list of questions, and that is I heard there was an entire section of *Stranger in a Strange Land* which was never used.

Heinlein: Oh, there are big chunks of *all* my stories that have never been used because I cut them to the bone as much as possible.

Schulman: Specifically, I heard it was one telling Valentine Michael Smith's origins on Mars.

Heinlein: Oh, I've forgotten offhand just how much of that I cut out; I'd have to go back and look at my notes. I suppose somebody's been reading the archives down in the vaults at University of California?

Schulman: Uh, or—Is there a library nearby you in

Santa Cruz that has that?

Heinlein: University of California is my archivist and its nearest campus is just below me. They have a completist attitude and the very roughest of rough notes are saved just as carefully as the final drafts. Any story I'd finished with—at the time they set it up—I just turned everything over to them concerning that story.

Schulman: I hope, one of these days, to get down there and start reading it.

Heinlein: Well, I don't think it's too edifying because if I hadn't thought the stuff I left in was better than the stuff I left out, I wouldn't have done it that way.

Schulman: Okay, I can buy that.

Heinlein: However, people who are interested in such literary matters—which I'm not, especially—do dig into all these notes and correspondence and such. Now where are we?

Schulman: Question number eight. ["Of all your stories, which one did you enjoy writing the most? Who is your favorite character?"]

Heinlein: All right. Oh, those are two very different things. When I gave the James Forrestal Memorial Lecture down there at the Naval Academy I answered specifically that first question. I enjoy writing them *all* because the thumb-rule that I have about fiction is whether of not it interests *me*. If it interests me then I assume that it probably will interest some other people. If it bores me I don't write it. Follow me?

Schulman: Okay.

Heinlein: And consequently: "Which one did you enjoy writing the most?" I enjoyed writing *all* of them or I would not have written them! Perhaps I enjoyed a little less the stories at the earlier part of my career when I was really bucking for money—when I needed the money badly. Nevertheless I enjoyed doing it even then.

Schulman: Okay.

Heinlein: You know that's an impossible thing for me to answer? To begin with, *all* an author's characters are the author himself speaking in one way or another. He may even be speaking as the Devil's Advocate at one point, but nevertheless the author does it all. I *could* say Lazarus Long but that would simply be because it's the character that's been on my mind most recently. I could equally handily say Podkayne Fries, or Rhysling—it doesn't matter. I *can't* have a favorite character. It's as ridiculous—If an author has a favorite character, why he'll behave like a parent with a favorite child. Each one has to be my favorite when I'm writing about him.

Schulman: Okay.

Heinlein: Or I don't do myself or the reader justice.

Schulman: All right. Why don't we skip along to number nine, then? ["New Libertarian Notes Review Editor Richard Friedman created a fictional list of books that Dr. Samuel Russell (a character in *Have Space Suit Will Travel*, for them who don't know) gave to Kip to supplement his education. It was printed in *NLN* 5 (Summer Issue, 1971) and I'm enclosing a Xerox copy for you. Interestingly enough, one of the books is Eric Temple Bell's *Men of Mathematics*, which you recommended to me just yesterday. Do you have any comments or additions?"]

From *NEW LIBERTARIAN NOTES* #5, Summer, 1971 (as reprinted in *NLN* #32)

"Reading List of Dr. Samuel Russell"
"obtained" by Richard A. Friedman

This is the promised list of books that Dr. Samuel Russell gave his son Kip so that he might acquire the education he was not getting in school. It is not a list of the best books ever written, although it contains some of them, nor indeed a canon of any kind, but simply books that Dr. Russell thought that Kip should read and study. The availability of books to the individual is a better educator than the enforcement of schooling on the masses. So here's an alternative to high school:

MATHEMATICS

9th Year Math—Sam Jaffee (yes, *that* Sam Jaffee)
11th Year Math—AMSCO Books
Plane Geometry—Barnett Rich
Analytical Geometry—Lehman
Men of Mathematics—Eric Temple Bell (John Taine)
An Introduction to Calculus—Kline

CHEMISTRY

Vitalized Chemistry—(AMSCO, I think)
General Chemistry—Thomas L. Brown
Orgasmic Chemistry—Morrison and Boyd
Physical Chemistry—Walter J. Moore (Ref.)
Biochemistry and Human Metabolism—Walker,
    Boyd, and Haber
Space Medicine—Asimov
Extraterrestrial Medicine—Stapp
Space Medicine—Struchold (Those four were given
    to him by Mr. Charton, the pharmacist).
Necronomicon—Abdul al Hazred

PHYSICS

1,2,3,...Infinity—Gamow (It seems even Dr. Russell
    was at a loss to find a good introductory Physics
    book.)

BIOLOGY

(?)—T.H. Huxley and Wells
The New Intelligent Man's Guide to Science (Biology
    Sections)—Asimov

A subscription to *Bio Notes*, Room 822, Main Building, New York University, Washington Square, New York, NY 10003

ASTRONOMY
Intelligent Life in the Universe—Shklovsky and Sagan

ECONOMICS
Economics—Samuelson
Capital—Marx
On Function—Dekker
Human Action—Von Mises

HISTORY
The Outline of History—Wells
The Story of Civilization—Will & Ariel Durant
The Oxford History of the American People—Samuel
   Eliot Morrison

POLITICS
The Republic—Plato
Second Treatise on Civil Government—Locke
The Declaration of Independence—Jefferson
The Constitution of the United States
The Prince—Machiavelli
Atlas Shrugged—Rand
The Moon is a Harsh Mistress and *Starship
   Troopers*—Heinlein

BIOGRAPHY

The Apology, Crito, Phaedo—Plato

FICTION

The Lord of the Rings—Tolkien
Don Quixote—Cervantes

POETRY AND DRAMA

The Iliad—Homer
Songs of Innocence and Experience—Blake
Theban Plays: *Oedipus, Oedipus at Colonus,*
   Antigone—Sophocles
King Lear—Shakespeare
Man and Superman—Shaw

FOUR GENERAL GUIDES TO LITERATURE

The back of any issue of *Classics Illustrated*
Good Reading—Signet Books
The Story of the World's Literature—John Macy
(HIGHEST POSSIBLE RECOMMENDATION)
Towards a Theory of Science Fiction—John J. Pierce

Heinlein: Let's see. I haven't had time to study that list; I know that about half of them were books I've read and about half were books I've not read but looked as if they might be appropriate. I haven't read *Have Space Suit — Will Travel* for quite a long time; does Dr. Russell give a specific list in there or not?

Schulman: No.

Heinlein: He doesn't? Well, I really haven't had time to study Friedman's list and since I haven't read about half of them I don't know. It looks as though it were a pretty good list. In any case, if a man just reads and keeps on reading, whether he reads my favorites or not he's going to broaden his education. As long as he reads *everything*. That's why I was urging you to read Eric Temple Bell.

Schulman: I've made a note to get my hands on both those books [Heinlein had also recommended Bell"s *Queen of The Sciences*] plus John J. Pierce made a Xerox copy of part of his *Development of Mathematics* dealing with epistemology.

Heinlein: Well, that's good. I recommended Eric Temple Bell because he's so very readable. In that same connection John R. Pierce—John J. Pierce's father—is one of the best popular expositors—in addition to being a fine research man; one of the great physicists of our day—he's one of the best popular expositors, just as Eric Temple Bell was. Oh, look up stuff by John R. Pierce with popular titles; he can give you an appreciation of mathematical physics—or at least certain aspects of it—that you can't get from ordinary study. Dr. Pierce is a very, very clever writer. I commend his popular works to your attention—not his technical works because he works in an extremely technical field. But his popular exposition of what he does—and what Claude [E.] Shannon does, for example—the originator of information theory?—this is good. Dr. Pierce for the applications of mathematics to physics—are very good sources.

Now, let's see.

Schulman: Well, we already went through ten and eleven.

Heinlein: Yes, all right now, twelve. "What is science fiction?" [(I define it as the sort of stuff Robert Heinlein writes.)]" Ah, yes. As you know, everybody takes a whack at that every now and then. Have you seen a book—just a moment, I'll catch the name; it's across the room here—[Long pause]—a book called *The Science Fiction Novel*, which contains four lectures—one by me, one by Alfred Bester, one by Cyril Kornbluth, and one by somebody else; I've forgotten who now— University of Chicago.

Schulman: I've heard it referred to. I haven't seen it.

Heinlein: Well, the name of it's *The Science Fiction Novel* and it's Advent Press. I discuss the nature of science fiction quite extensively in the opening part of my lecture, and inasmuch as it's there and in print and you can unquestionably get it out of the library, I'll let it go with this one remark here: Science fiction is to my mind—if you want to separate it from fantasy—science fiction is based on the real world, speculation that takes place—usually into the future—about the real world, and which takes science as a necessary aspect of the story that you're writing—meaning if you left the science out the story would fall to pieces. Fantasy, on the other hand, is a fairy-tale for grown-ups. It is not based on the real world. This is no criticism of fantasy; I'm not opposed to it at all. Tolkien's "Ring" trilogy, for example, is fantasy, laid in an unreal world about unreal things; that doesn't keep it from having philosophical importances to it that many students have seen. I write both science fiction *and* fantasy and I sometimes mix them up in the same story in a way that purists do not like. You have read *Glory Road*?

Schulman: One of my favorites.

Heinlein: Well, that's both science fiction and fantasy all mixed up together.

Schulman: I've been thinking for years that a story, for instance, like *Between Planets*—I could see it very easily shifted into an eighteenth or nineteenth century mode, you know, written by somebody like Robert Louis Stevenson, and instead of having Don Harvey being born between planets he could be born on a ship between countries...

Heinlein: Yes, yes. However, it was hard-core science fiction for its time because at the time I wrote that story it was still conceivable that Venus could be that sort of planet. That was written before we knew anything about Venus, or what we knew about it was the small amount that we could learn from the surface of this planet. I have written stories that are outright fantasies, such as "The Unpleasant Profession of Jonathan Hoag." Now you can't by any stretch of the imagination call that science fiction; there isn't any science in it and one simply goes along with the assumptions in it long enough to read the story. Or a story such as my short story—it was about city politics and a reporter and it involved a whirlwind that seemed to be setting it—I've forgotten the name of the story right now; it's in the same collection with "Jonathan Hoag"—that's a fantasy. ["Our Fair City" in *6 x H*—JNS] In fact, that entire collection with "Jonathan Hoag" are pretty much fantasies—"The Man Who Traveled In Elephants"; that's about all you can call that. All I can say about it is that I try to know which I'm doing when I'm doing it. There are a lot of people writing science fiction who don't know anything about science and they *think* they're writing science fiction when actually they're writing nonsense...[Quoting question:] "Are any of your books *not* science fiction by your definition?" Yes, and you can pretty well pick them out in addition to the ones I've named. Well, "Magic Incorporated" is an example of one that is definitely fantasy, not science fiction.

Schulman: But you would say that "Waldo" *is* science fiction?

Heinlein: It's closer to being fantasy but it has some

science fiction aspects. As with *Glory Road*, I mixed the two elements into one story, which the purists don't care for, but sometime you can tell a good story that way. As far as I'm concerned, fiction is intended to entertain. If I can manage to entertain with it, that's what the cash customer is paying for. So I don't hesitate to write straight science fiction, straight fantasy, or a mixture of the two—or *anything* else. I've written all sorts of things. I've written first person, teenage *female* love stories laid in the present—not science fiction at all, but the sort of thing that I sold to girls' magazines, girls' teenage magazines—one magazine was called *Senior Prom.*

Schulman: What name did you write under?

Heinlein: Now, that's a nasty question.

Schulman: [Laughing] I'm really interested. [It never occurred to me that Heinlein would publish outside his own genre under his own name — and a *male* name; he had regularly used pen names early in his career when writing fantasy. I was merely looking for the name he was using on those stories so I could search them out. But what I didn't know is that Heinlein's "Puddin'" stories (later published in *Expanded Universe*) were published under the byline "R.A. Heinlein." — JNS, 1999]

Heinlein: Look, those stories were written quite some

time ago; their only importance was that they were sufficiently entertaining to be entertaining to teenage girls. I did it more or less experimentally because I had a female editor who said it couldn't be *done*. Whereupon I did it. Whereupon I finally thereafter started putting some female, teenage lead characters into my science fiction: "The Menace From Earth," for example; that's a piece of hard-core science fiction but the lead character is a fifteen, sixteen year old girl. Told in the first person, do you remember that story—"The Menace From Earth"?

Schulman: Very, very well.

Heinlein: That was a direct result of having done those teenage love stories. And, eventually, I did *Podkayne of Mars* and there are two or three others kicking around here and there. I started using realistic female characters thereafter because I found it fleshed the stories out, it seemed to improve them.

Schulman: Tell me, does the name "Lazabee Green" mean anything to you?

Heinlein: The name what?

Schulman: Lazabee Green.

Heinlein: Spell it.

Schulman: L-A-Z-A-B-E-E.

Heinlein: Lazadee?

Schulman: Lazabee, with a "b" as in Betty.

Heinlein: Yes.

Schulman: Green.

Heinlein: Greed.

Schulman: G-R-E-E-N.

Heinlein: Green. Lazabee Green. I don't believe I've ever read a story about such a character and I don't think I've known such person.

Schulman: There was a rumor going around that this was one of your pen-names.

Heinlein: [Laughing] Oh. No, it's not. It doesn't mean anything to me at all. I can assure that this is *not* one of my pen-names.

Schulman: Okay.

Heinlein: [Chuckling] A long time past I was accused of having the pen-name of L. Ron Hubbard, but that was many, many years ago.

Schulman: [Laughing] It doesn't seem likely now.

Heinlein: Oh, it used to amuse Ron. We'd talk it over from time to time.

Schulman: Okay. I guess we might as well move on to thirteen.

Heinlein: Question thirteen? Oh, but on twelve; "Do you prefer the term 'speculative' fiction? If so, why?" Yes, I prefer the term "speculative" fiction because there isn't anything about *that* term which ties me down to putting a lot of atomic physics or such into a story. It's a looser term. More elbow room. Speculation about the future. But serious speculation.

Now thirteen, ["About your future writing plans. Do you intend to write another juvenile? How about a story taking place (perhaps this wishful thinking on my part) in a working anarcho-capitalist society with competing private police, arbitration, and armies?"] Future writing plans, we've already discussed that somewhat. If I continue to live and have a reasonable amount of health, I'll probably write some stories. I couldn't guess what they might be. For the past few years I've been ill as much as I've been well, so I haven't gotten very much done. As of right now I don't know what my next story will be.

Schulman: Okay. I could tell you right off, though, that there are a lot of libertarian fans who would be quite happy to see you write something along the lines I described in number thirteen.

Heinlein: Well, I'll write it if it strikes me as a good story. I won't write it if not. If it's simply going to be a lecture, no. If I see a really good story in it, I would tackle it. I don't know; I've got things like that in the file. I did *something* like that in *Podkayne of Mars* when I took them to Venus. You remember that Venus had no government as such it simply had capitalists and employees and tourists.

Schulman: Right, but there was only *one* company which I'm not sure is what normally would develop.

Heinlein: I'm not sure it is, either. But I say I did *something* like that once.

Schulman: Okay.

Heinlein: L. Sprague De Camp did something like that with lots of companies; it was called "The Stolen Dormouse."

Schulman: I'll have to look that up.

Heinlein: It's in a book of his—[Away from telephone;] (Yes, sweetheart.) It's in a—I can't remember what the title of the book was. I *should* remember; it was dedicated to me, but a good many years back. The title—

Oh, *Divide and Rule* was the title of the volume, but I think it included "The Stolen Dormouse." It was in *Astounding* along about 1940, something like that. It described the United States under circumstances where everything was run by a bunch of *competing* corporations. It was quite amusing. Now, fourteen?

Schulman: Fourteen.

Heinlein: "Do you believe that a 'romantic' story necessarily involves highly motivated characters striving —" Look, that's the sort of question you ask a professor of English! [Laughter] I'm not a literary person; I just write stories. They're intended to amuse people. I'm not sure what the difference is between a "romantic" story and some other sort of story, I've written stories that involved "highly motivated characters striving for a single, overpowering goal beset with obstacles and antagonists until the climatic resolution"—I have done that, yes. "Is this the story you like to read? Like to write? Used to like?" Look, I read *everything*. I'm a *garbage paper* reader. I'm the type of a person who sits on the curbstone and opens up paper wet from garbage to read the continuation of the jump page! I gave you my only thumb-rule for a story; if it interests *me*—if *I* find it interesting—I'll write it on the assumption that somebody else will be interested in it, too, but if it bores me I won't write it. But all of these other things, these are things that professors of English talk about in courses on literature and that's simply not the sort of education I had. If I had started worrying about things like that when I started writing I probably wouldn't have written even one story.

Schulman: Okay.

Heinlein: Fifteen, we've had that, haven't we?

Schulman: Right, and I think we've pretty much covered sixteen, too. [Question seventeen was irrelevant at this point.] I guess we're up to eighteen then.

Heinlein: "Do you see many of your recent story endings as downbeat? If so/not, why?" Well, I don't see them as downbeat. Do you? If so, which ones?

Schulman: Well, I found *The Moon Is a Harsh Mistress* a bit depressing—from my point of view.

Heinlein: [Chuckling] Because the perfect anarchy wasn't set up as a result of it?

Schulman: Right. [Also for a rather obvious reason which didn't come to mind; both my favorite characters—Mycroft and Prof—were dead (or presumed dead) at the end.] Or because you seemed to feel government was an inevitable "disease."

Heinlein: I'm not sure that it's inevitable but I see nothing in the history of the human race to indicate to me that it is *not*.

Schulman: You gotta start *somewhere*.

Heinlein: I'm not disagreeing with that, either. Let's see, the expression "necessary evil" was from Thomas Jefferson, wasn't it?

Schulman: I don't know, specifically. [I have since learned that it's from the opening of Thomas Paine's "Common Sense."]

Heinlein: I think it was from Thomas Jefferson who was certainly a libertarian of his period. I never thought of *Harsh Mistress* as being downbeat. There are indications quite early in the story that they're *not* going to wind up with an anarchy, they simply *aren't*; you can see that from the fashion in which the committee starts to organize. I don't mean the revolutionary committee, but after they've taken over and they're trying to hold things together.

Schulman: Several of your stories that have sort of dismissed the idea of finding a final resolution to philosophical problems on earth I find a little depressing because—

Heinlein: Oh, oh! Well, yes, I can make some comment

---

* I didn't realize how funny this aside was until I became a published author myself. — JNS, 1999.

on that. Clear back in a thing called *Sixth Column*—which is a story that I wrote to a plot of John Campbell's and didn't particularly want to write, except that I needed the money—I added a lot of things into it that John Campbell didn't have in his plot including the idea that there *were* no final solutions. And Neil, there aren't.

Schulman: Well, that won't prevent me from looking for them.

Heinlein: Yes, but don't be too discouraged when you don't find them. My wife—who is only a little younger than I am—still looks for these final answers, and is still hopeful. I got over looking for final solutions a good, long time ago because once you get this point shored up, something breaks out somewhere else. The human race gets along by the skin of its teeth, and it's been doing so for some hundreds of thousands or millions of years. Human solutions are *never* final solutions—at least so far as the history of the race up to now indicates. When I was a kid we had the "War to End All Wars"—going to make the world "safe for democracy." Now look at the damn thing. In fact, all you needed to do was take a little over ten years after that war as over and things were already in bad shape. We thought we had all the problems of our economy solved except the problems of distribution—I'm talking about the race as a whole, I'm not talking about my books*—and now we suddenly discover that we're in a closed spaceship, a goldfish bowl, and if we don't get a balanced aquarium we're going to poison ourselves with our own poisons. It is the common human condition all through history that every time you solve a problem you discover that you've also created a *new* problem. I *did* a story based on this called *Beyond This Horizon*—

Schulman: Which I'm just rereading, now.

Heinlein: All right. I started out with the assumption that *all* present-day problems had been solved at that point. I describe a utopia—largely anarchistic; there isn't enough government there to matter—and what do we do? We've got a hero who says: "Nevertheless, it ain't worth the trouble! What's it all about?" *He's* unhappy in this utopia simply because he doesn't have those answers to noumena—that I defined earlier?— the problems of philosophy known as noumena. And he finally accepts—agrees to accept—a partial answer: that a serious research effort will be undertaken—not to solve all those problems but simply to find out whether or not there is life after death, because that would— whether the answer is yes or whether the answer is no—it would affect the final answers on other things.

Schulman: Do you have any opinions on that question?

Heinlein: I usually do not express them in newspapers.

Schulman: Off the record?

Heinlein: I have little or no objective data. So far as *subjective* data is concerned, I *incline* to the notion that when we die, we don't die all over. That we do *not* die all over. That there is *something* that persists. But even that—because that opens up all of the questions of philosophy and religion—I avoid discussing other than in fiction. You'll find it discussed in fiction endlessly, both in this last book and in *Stranger in a Strange Land* and *Beyond This Horizon* and lots of others.

Schulman: I'll repeat the comment that I made in my letter; that I think religion and politics—or "philosophy" and politics—are the only subjects worth arguing about.

Heinlein: Well, yes. There are four major subjects as mentioned by Lazarus Long: war, money, politics, and love—and matters of philosophy affect all four of those. Those are four principal interests of the human animal. Sex, economic motivation, war, and politics. Politics in its broadest sense, which would include anarchy.

Schulman: Right. Without meaning to get back on the subject of libertarianism again—because we *can't* go very far on that—I just wanted to make the comment that *Podkayne of Mars* there's a whole speech by Uncle Tom about not putting down politics because it's the way men get along without fighting

Heinlein: Yes.

Schulman: Well, we're in agreement about the idea of getting along without fighting, it's just that I—again using Franz Oppenheimer's definition—would call that the *economic* method, rather than the *political* method.

Heinlein: Well, politics simply names a field, that's all. Politics is the whole field of human interrelations. It is so difficult to separate the economic and the political factors that the subjects are often lumped in together as political economy—one title.

   Now, let's see.

Schulman: I guess we're up to nineteen or twenty; both are basically the same question. [Question nineteen, asking for an expansion of Heinlein's views on Ayn Rand, was dispensed with as having too low a priority for the *Sunday News*.]

Heinlein: Twenty: "What philosophers or artists—past or present—attract you, and why?"

Schulman: That's a big question.

Heinlein: Well, yes it is...I studied philosophy under Will Durant many, many years ago—this was before he was well-known, *long* before he was well-known; this was back in the early twenties—and he first introduced me to a wide range of philosophers; and I read 'em all; I gobbled 'em all. I suppose I've learned something from all of them, but not necessarily what they wanted to impart. It took me quite a while, for example, to realize that what Plato was preaching was the direct opposite of what I liked and believed in—[Laughter]—because it was so well-told, so well-expressed. Artists?—are you speaking of pictorial art, or what?

Schulman: I'm using art in the very general categories of music, painting, literature...

Heinlein: My tastes in art are pretty eclectic. I refer you to some remarks by Dr. Jubal Harshaw in *Stranger In a Strange Land* in which he discuses art and in which he indicates that most of the artists he likes are pre-World War One—and why. Now, this is not entirely true of myself—there are a lot of good artists around—but I'm reminded of something a Norwegian artist told me in Oslo a good many years ago. I asked him what he thought of American artists—did we have any good artists at the present time?—and he said, "Oh, yes, yes—you've got lots of them. But they're all in *commercial* art. [Laughter] This is a period when a great many of the so-called fine artists are apparently painting with old brooms, and would be horrified at the idea that a picture actually had to *look* like something? Or say anything to the viewer? I'm an old square on that; I want to be able to understand a picture that I look at.

Schulman: My father still has a color slide of three huge, white canvasses at the Museum of Modern Art with absolutely *nothing* on them.

Heinlein: Yes. Did your father like that?

Schulman: He thought it was a big joke.

Heinlein: Yes, I think so, too. Like that pianist here some years back at one of these far out things who gave a concert that consisted of going to the piano and sitting there holding perfectly still for twelve minutes. Never touched the keys.

Schulman: Yes, this was just done in Boston within the past two years.

Heinlein: Yes. That's carrying a joke a bit far; however, if they can get away with it, it's all right with me; I simply won't subscribe to it.

Schulman: Well, you might pay for it once just for the gimmick, but I doubt that you'll ask for the recording.

Heinlein: Have you read *Huckleberry Finn*?

Schulman: Not for a long time.

Heinlein: Well, do you remember that the Duke and the Dauphin arranged a show down in Arkansas that was a phony, a fake? And they put on three performances; the first, the people were dismayed; the second one, they had everybody else in town because the first people attending wouldn't admit they'd been swindled; and the third night, everybody showed up and they were carrying rotten eggs and dead cats and so forth. The Duke and the Dauphin snuck out the back door with the receipts and were half way to the river before Huck realized that they were about to go off without him! [Laughter] Mark Twain defined in there how many times you can get away with a swindle, and in that particular case three times—as long as you risk being lynched.

Schulman: Okay.

Heinlein: Now. let's see. [Reading question twenty-one] "One of your main themes has constantly stressed that man is the most dangerous, deadly, and resourceful beast in the universe. Do you believe this? [If so, since we have no basis of comparison as yet, why?]"

Look, we aren't off this planet yet, really. I don't know whether he is or he isn't. Actually, what I'm saying at that point is he's the most dangerous, deadly, and resourceful beast on *this* planet, because that is all the universe we know so far. He certainly is on this planet—of course we've only been dominant for a relatively short time; the returns from upstate are not in yet—[Laughter]—but as of right now, we are just that. I kept emphasizing that because there are so many people going around talking sweetness and light, acting as if the human animal—all you needed to do was make sure that you petted him enough when he's a small child and then he would never bite. I don't believe it. We got this way—we got where we are—over the course of a long stretch of evolution, by being survivor types in a very tough jungle. And from all I've seen of the human race so far, they're still that mean, tough, and nasty. I do not mean that as a derogatory remark, either; I think that's what it takes *to* survive. That doesn't mean you have to be mean, tough, and nasty in your daily behavior. In other words, I am not a pacifist, and I do not think the human animal is put together so he can *be* a pacifist and still survive. Pacifists stay alive at the present time because others who are not pacifists have put up with them and protect them in spite of themselves. There are some indications of that in *Time Enough For Love*, too. My ideal on that would be Dora in "The Tale of the Adopted Daughter" who's shown as utterly sweet and gentle all the way through except the one time when she was called upon to shoot and she shot. Did it right, and didn't hesitate.

Schulman: I think I'm going to have to transfer cassettes at this point. One second.

Heinlein: All right.
[AFTER NEW CASSETTE IS PUT IN]

Schulman: Okay, I guess we're up to number twenty-two, now.

Heinlein: All right. Hold it just a second. On twenty-one: One of the reasons I have emphasized that is because there have been lots of other writers who have always talked as if just as soon as we got in touch with really intelligent, highly advanced races, we will find them to be peaceful vegetarians. Well, I don't think that is necessarily true at all. There's no data on which to base that; it is simply wishful thinking on the part of the writers who write that way. The universe might turn out to be a hell of a sight nastier and tougher place than we have any reason to guess at this point. That first contact just *might* wipe out the human race, because we would encounter somebody who was meaner and tougher, and not at all inclined to be bothered by genocide. Be no more bothered by genocide than I am when I put out ant poison in the kitchen when the ants start swarming in.

Schulman: Do you think any of the U.F.O's have been actual contacts?

Heinlein: I don't know. I simply don't have data.

Schulman: What about Air Force Project *Bluebook*?

Heinlein: I don't have data. There have been some ooh-foh sightings that are extremely hard to explain. I'm reminded of something Willy Ley said to me, oh, twenty, twenty-five years ago. He said: "Vun. Dere is something dere. Two. I do not know vat it iss." I'm just about where Willy Ley put it then; there is something there and I do not know what it is.

Schulman: Okay. [Question number twenty-two; "Alexei Panshin in *Heinlein In Dimension* claims that Clark Fries is 'thoroughly sick.' Since Clark happens to be one of my favorite characters, I believe Panshin is wrong, and that whatever Clark's problems, his natural intelligence will finally resolve them. What do you think?"]

Heinlein: Number twenty-two; I have not read *Heinlein in Dimension*; I've never seen it.

Schulman: Okay.

Heinlein: Clark Fries—his *uncle* indicates in the very end of the story that he thinks the boy is sadly in need of treatment, yes. That's the uncle's opinion. And he also thinks the boy got into the shape that he's in through being neglected by his parents. That is the opinion of the uncle, however, I can see how Mr. Panshin would reach that opinion. You say that he happens to be one of your favorite characters. Well, he's one of *my* favorite characters, too. He was quite a lot of fun to write. Instead of writing the sweet, little Boy Scouts that I've done so many times, I wrote a character who was strictly self-centered. "And his natural intelligence will finally resolve"—yes, the last paragraph of the book indicates that Clark Fries had decided to join the human race. Yes, I would agree with you on that. He's *quite* young, you know, he's what?—twelve years old, something like that? And to expect much in the way of social integration out of a twelve-year-old is to be sadly disappointed.

Schulman: Okay.

Heinlein: He's growing up, though. Yes. And he's quite intelligent.

[Number twenty-three:] "Are you familiar with the psychological theories of Dr. Thomas Szasz?" I have in my study one of his books which I've read. Let me see the name of it here, if I can read it from across the room. The general idea was that he's opposed to psychiatry—although he's a professor or psychiatry—he's opposed to psychiatry as it's organized *now*. *The Myth of Mental Illness*, that's it.

Schulman: The main point I was referring to here is his basic idea that you have to define mental illness— You just can't say that because someone commits an abhorrent act that he's "sick"; he says that the medical analogy just doesn't hold up.

Heinlein: That's right.

Schulman: And you seemed to be making a similar point with the "sound semantic orientation" in "Coventry."

Heinlein: Yes, somewhat. Not the identical point, but a somewhat similar point. As far as I'm concerned the defense in court of "Not Guilty By Reason Of Insanity" should not be considered a defense at all. But, I'm not a psychiatrist.

Schulman: I guess what I'm referring to next is the question: "If a person understands the consequences of 'damaging' another...[(namely, Rothbardian theory, full restitution to the victim plus cost of apprehension and interest for the time lost; or in the case of murder the murderer becomes the slave of the victim's heirs), isn't his psychological state irrelevant?"]

Heinlein: Look, that's a very complex question, particularly in that you want me to take a high order abstraction and follow that abstraction by somebody else's intensional definition, rather than an extensional definition. [These are terms used in General Semantics. Ordinary philosophers would use the term "lexical" where Heinlein was using "intensional"; and "ostensive" where Heinlein was using "extensional."—JNS, 1999]

Schulman: I looked those up, and I'd like to be sure I understand them.

Heinlein: Extensional is where you define the word "chair" by pointing to a half a dozen or a dozen or twenty different chairs, and add; "and many others." That's an *extensional* definition. An extensional definition of human beings would be to go down and point to any busload and add; "and many others." Now an intensional definition is a definition you'll find in words in a dictionary. An intensional definition is where you define one symbol by means of other symbols. An extensional definition is where you define a symbol by its referrents. The referent of the symbol. Korzybski, in lecturing, used to do away with any discussion of religion right at that point by inviting anyone in the audience to define the word "God"—G-o-d—and insisting that they define it *extensionally*, not define it in terms of other symbols. Try pointing at God.

Schulman: Yes. Well, I remember when I was five years old—I was going home with my mother after we'd been out shopping, or something like that—and I asked her: "Where is God?" And since she was unable to tell me, from that point on I said, "Well gee. If she doesn't know where it is then how does she know there is one?"

Heinlein: Yes. Well, Korzybski's point was that since you can't point to the referent for this symbol, we are not prepared to engage in any further discussion of it.

Schulman: Was Korzybski trying to make the point that there was very little use for intensional definitions?

Heinlein: Well, there's a thing called the "Semantic Rosary" that he used to use—levels of abstraction. If you read this book *Science and Sanity*—or better yet, much easier to read is Dr. S.I. Hayakawa's *Language In*

Action; the revised edition has slightly different wording [*Language in Thought and Action*—JNS, 1999] but if you look that up you'd find the revised edition, too— This Hayakawa that I'm speaking of is the one that settled the riots at San Francisco State [College, not Prison].

Schulman: I remember that.

Heinlein: He's quite a boy; mind you, this is a man older than *I* am who faced sown those rioters with his bare hands—and stopped the riots. He's not much older than I am, but he is a bit. I knew him first oh forty, yes forty, years ago.

Schulman: I see reference to him in your 1941 Worldcon speech [Heinlein's Guest of Honor speech, "The Discovery of the Future"].

Heinlein: I referred to Hayakawa?

Schulman: Mm, hmm.

Heinlein: Well, that's good, so that—He's been around for a while. He's no chicken. And his stuff is much easier to read than Korzybski's; Korzybski was a Pole, and I've never seen a Pole yet writing in English who didn't manage to get pretty turgid. Korzybski was a wonderful lecturer but his writing is rather difficult to follow, even though he is a s[S]emanticist. [Laughter]

You can almost see him translating in his head. Hayakawa—despite his Japanese name—speaks English as a native language; he learned it as a baby in Canada, so that Hayakawa handles English much more easily than Korzybski ever did. I commend it your attention.

Schulman: Okay.

Heinlein: But don't miss Korzybski before you're through. Korzybski is the fountainhead; Hayakawa is the follower.

Schulman: In other words, Hayakawa brought Korzybski down to earth?

Heinlein: Somewhat like that. Certainly Hayakawa handles English in such a fashion that the layman can read it, whereas Korzybski is heavy going—quite technical.

Now where are we on this: Dr. Szasz…"damaging"… "isn't his psychological state irrelevant?" As I say, that involves so much in the way of high abstraction that I wouldn't attempt to answer it on my feet. [Quoting the last part of twenty-three:] "Isn't "Coventry" still an attempt by the state (albeit a relatively benign one) to interfere with the natural market processes and not let the victim have his restitution?" Well, "Coventry" was an attempt on the part of a writer to make a few hundred dollars to pay off a mortgage. [Laughter] I got an idea for a quite different way of treating violations of law from the method of either hanging them or throwing them into jail. Simply divorce them, that's all. Expel them from society. And I still think it has its points although all I tried to make out of it was a novelette, and certainly there are lots of other things that can be said about it.

Schulman: I specifically, however, remember "Coventry" as the first time which I pointed to a story and said, "Yeah, this is pretty much what I've been trying to say about the type of society I wanted to live in; and that's the story that—even though I didn't know the term at that point—I became a libertarian on.

Heinlein: Mm,hmmm. Number twenty-four next?

Schulman: I guess so.

Heinlein: "Madalyn Murray O'Hair once told me that she's read everything you've ever written. [Any comments?]" I don't have any comment on that; I don't know the lady; I have never met her. I think I read an article—an interview—about her in the *Saturday Evening Post* about twenty years ago, and that's all. I really don't know very much about her. I'm pleased to hear she's read everything I've ever written; the more of those we have around, the more money I make.

Schulman: I tend to think there are quite a few. I know

at least twenty who can make that claim.

Heinlein: Well, inasmuch as I started in this business to make money and my purpose was to entertain, why this pleases me. I don't know Mrs. O'Hair—or "Ms." O'Hair, or whatever she calls herself—I really know nothing at all about her except that every now and then she takes part in a class action case and it always seems to be libertarian.

Schulman: Okay.

I've managed to whip up a few more questions that aren't on the pages I've given you ; let's see if I can get a couple of them out of the way. John J. Pierce gave me a few questions which he wanted to know [and which I asked because I *also* was interested in them]…He wants me to ask you if you're aware that many who admire your work up to *The Moon Is a Harsh Mistress* or so are turned off by *I Will Fear No Evil* and *Time Enough For Love* and he's wondering if you think you've changed that much.

Heinlein: No, I do not. I knew that he was turned off by both of those books; he let me know…Probably John Jeremy would be considerably disappointed to know that *I Will Fear No Evil* was listed as a bestseller last year in a publishers' publication comparing the sales of the whole market; I think it would distress him. I got some bad reviews primarily inside science fiction itself; I got good reviews from outside science fiction and the book has been extremely successful with the public, whether it's popular with John Jeremy or not.

Schulman: I think what he's trying to say —and I've gotten similar things from several other of my friends— is that they seem to feel that it's not as quite "hard core" science fiction.

Heinlein: Yes, yes. I have departed from the "true religion." [Laughter] Yes, I know. I remember a letter I received—oh, it must have been around 1947 for it was shortly after I had my first story published in the *Saturday Evening Post*; the story was "The Green Hills of Earth"—and it was from someone, a reader of *Astounding* chewing me out for departing from hard-core science fiction and also casting me into the outer darkness for going over into the slicks instead of staying with *Astounding*. I didn't even bother to answer the letter. The *Saturday Evening Post* was paying me something like ten times the word-rate that *Astounding* did; I couldn't *afford* to write for *Astounding* on that basis. I am happy to say that the public liked the book that he [J.J. Pierce] disliked so much, and I am also happy to say that I'm getting excellent reviews on this new book.

Schulman: Did you read my review, yet?

Heinlein: I glanced through it rather hastily.

Schulman: Was there anything you strongly disagreed

with of anything I said?

Heinlein: No. No, I didn't. It seemed to me the review was quite fair. You did mention the difference in pacing—that's true. When you're writing an adventure story you *do* pace it differently from this sort of story, however there are adventure sequences in *Time Enough For Love* that *are* paced pretty fast—here and there—but it is not primarily an adventure story. In fact it's a whole bunch of stories, that's true. But how are you going to cope with twenty-three centuries in one book?

Schulman: With great difficulty?

Heinlein: [Laughing] Yes...Over the course of some thirty-four years of writing, every now and then I receive things from people condemning me for not having written a story just like my last one. I never pay any attention to this, Neil, because it has been my intention—my purpose—to make every story I've written different from every *other* story I've ever written—never to write a story just like my last one...I'm going to write what it suits me to write and if I write another story that's like any other story I've ever written, I'll be slipping.

Schulman: I have a note up on my wall which I look at whenever I start getting down because somebody doesn't like a story I've written and it says something along the line of: "I'll write what I want to write, how I want to write, and for whatever reason I want to write it, and if anybody doesn't like it, he can go 'censored' for all I care."

Heinlein: Well, inasmuch as I have always written with the reader in mind, I agree with all of that but add onto it that I write for publication things that I think people will enjoy reading...and this book *I Will Fear No Evil* has been extremely successful with the general public, whether or not it appeals to a small group of science fictions fans...I'm trying to write to please not even as few as forty thousand people in the hardcover, but a million and up on the softcover. If an author let these self-appointed mentors decide for him what he's going to write and how he's going to write it, he'd never get anywhere...

Schulman: It has been suggested to me that since I'm writing for a paper like the *Sunday News* I should do a sort of "movie-star"-type interview and ask you questions like "What are your hobbies? Do you have a garden?" That sort of thing.

Heinlein; Well, if you want to know things of that sort. I used to alternate writing books with stonemasonry when I was in good health; I'm no longer physically up to that. But I've done a lot of stonemasonry and general mechanic work. I can do almost any of the construction trades. Of course I'm an engineer by training, but I'm pretty handy with almost any tools. I can wire a house or set a toilet or almost anything of that sort—the sort of work with his hands that I described Lazarus Long as doing, these were things I know how to do. My wife is very much of a gardener, but I don't garden myself. At the present time what with frequent illnesses it's about all I can do to manage to keep up with the nonfiction that I have to keep up with to know what's going on. In consequence, I don't read very much fiction now—not because I don't want to but because I don't have time to. Reading science fiction back before I started writing it was my favorite way of spending leisure. But, Lordy, I don't have time to do it now. I do read a little of it, but not much. There are some very good writers around loose now whose work I have accumulated and hope to get to some time. Larry Niven, for example, is an example of a very good science fiction writer but I haven't read too much of his—I've simply got it accumulated in my room—just lack of time for I find Larry Niven *very* entertaining. Do you read him?

Schulman: I haven't read anything of his, yet.

Heinlein: Well, I commend him to your attention. He's a very creative writer and very clever. He writes a good yarn.

My wife and I for many years have traveled as much as we could; this has been somewhat held down by illness in the past four or five years. I've been to South America a couple of times in the last four years but that's about as far away as I've been. But for a number of years I'd write a story while she prepared another trip and then we'd take the trip and I'd write a story while she prepared another trip and then we'd take the trip and I'd come back and write another story. I've never written more than about three months out of the year the whole time I've been writing. Part of that is because I never rewrite. I cut, but I don't rewrite.

Schulman: I envy that. I rewrite [then, not now] everything I put my pen to at least ten times—not through desire, it's just through dissatisfaction.

Heinlein: Well, I never learned to do it that way. Far, far better to take it a little slower and write it the way you intend it to be and then I find I still have to take a brush-pen—and cut out unnecessary verbiage. Oh, I cut thirty or forty thousand words out of this last one, and I cut twenty-five, thirty thousand words out of what I thought was the final version of *Stranger in a Strange Land.* I mean I'd already cut it before that and then I cut out another twenty-five thousand words out of it to get it down to a manageable size.

Schulman; One thing I was wondering about; were those "omitted's" in *Time Enough For Love* places where you actually cut, or was it just an insert at that point?

Heinlein: In some cases they were actual cuts; in other cases they're simply abrupt transitions to make it faster. An example of the abrupt transition is once when I decided that the reader had had plenty of the hardships of getting that covered wagon through the pass, and I just cut out the next several weeks. That's simply an abrupt transition, in other cases I cut it out because—after having written it—I cut it out because it wasn't absolutely necessary and the book was too damn big already.

For years and years we've traveled, oh, around the world three times, and I don't know how many times to Europe, over the North Pole, four or five times to South America. We've covered just about all the globe that we could reach, in view of the fact that you couldn't get a visa for Red China, and I did avoid the Congo after things got tough in there—just plain too difficult to travel. And usually Mrs. Heinlein has learned to speak at least one of the local languages and in some cases, I have, too. She can speak eight languages—I can get along in four—but she's not a professional linguist, she's a biochemist specializing in tropical and sub-tropical plants, genetics of them. But she happens to have an ear for languages and she studies very hard, so there's at least three languages that she can think in and some eight languages that she can get along it. But when she finished NYU a good many years ago she had only three languages; she simply kept adding them on.

We're both very fond of dancing; we haven't done much of it lately. We used to do a lot of dancing on ice. We belonged to a couple of figure skating clubs that regularly had ice dancing—social dancing on ice. I don't know whether you've ever seen it but all of the usual dances that are done on boards can be done on skates. And we belonged to a square dancing club and a cotillion and one thing or another, but we're always set up for dancing here in the house. But you get older...so we just don't dance as much as we used to.

Schulman: Does your house resemble at all the description of Jubal Harshaw's place?

Heinlein: Well, of course I wrote that book when I was in Colorado—but not too much. Jubal Harshaw's house was tailored to Jubal; this house is tailored to us. It's an eccentric house in that it's as carefully tailored to us as a custom-made girdle. It's circular because Mrs. Heinlein wanted a circular house. I did the design work on it, but I did very largely what she wanted to accomplish. Got a big atrium in the middle of it—twelve feet across to the sky, open to the sky—which has a tree in it, and flowers. And it has all sorts of things that I put in to make housekeeping easier, for example everything is either built in or on wheels. One or the other. It's either built solid with the house or it's on wheels so it will roll, with the single exception of her baby grand. Putting a baby grand on wheels isn't too practical. Oh, and very complex wiring, and it's a forced-air factory system for ventilation and heating and so forth.

Schulman: Are you a high-fidelity buff at all?

Heinlein: Not particularly. We do have a hi-fi system but I'm not the sort of a hi-fi buff who's continually worrying about components and, "Look at this curve" and, "now let's turn the gain up high and see what you can get there" and, you know, where their interest is in reproduction. Our interest is in the music. And we have an excellent sound system which a hi-fi buff would probably be playing with all the time and changing around. We simply got an expert to put the thing in an then we use it to play music. We have speakers distributed all around the house and outdoors—I don't know, fifteen, sixteen speakers—with switches and pads to let us get any combination we want. And the swimming pool is arranged the same way—I mean automated. Automatic cleaning, automatic chlorinization, and so forth.

Schulman: I remember that—you just mentioned *Beyond This Horizon* a short time ago—in *Beyond This Horizon* is the first description I've ever seen of a waterbed. Do you have one of those?

Heinlein: I've got one but it's in the storehouse; I don't have any place to set it up. The first man to manufacture 'em sent us one as a compliment; he'd picked it up, not from *Beyond This Horizon*, but where I described it much more clearly in *Stranger in a Strange Land*. I designed the waterbed back in the thirties and couldn't afford to build the things. I wanted it then because I was an invalid. But I couldn't afford to build it and then finally used it in fiction, and a number of people picked it up from there and now *everybody's* building waterbeds. And some of them are built quite precisely to my specifications. I mean they really worked. Some of them are not so well-built. But I don't have space to set up a waterbed in this house without tearing something else out. And we do have some tailor made and quite comfortable beds.

The house has all sorts of things to make housekeeping simple because neither one of us cares too much for servants, and yet we've got a big enough place—and we're getting old enough—that we otherwise would need help. She has electronic cooking and, oh, little things. There are twelve or thirteen telephone jacks throughout the house, and eight or ten instruments so that no matter where we happen to be we can answer the phone there. And each of the bathrooms has a door to the outside so you can go directly from the bathroom to the pool without tracking wet and muddy feet through the house. A lot of things like that. It's an eccentric house, all right, but it's simply tailored to what we need to do.

Schulman: I remember in *The Door Into Summer* you went through quite a bit about the drudgery of housework and one of the premises of the story had to do with all sorts of devices to make it easier. Have you come up with any of those things?

Heinlein: Most of the things I described in there are so far out that they would be extremely expensive to develop. That electronic equipment and so forth. It can be done, sure, but it would not be easy. I haven't attempted to put anything of that sort into *this* house because you can't buy it off the shelf and I'm not equipped to do— nor do I have any inclination to do—the tremendous amount of R and D work that would be involved.

Schulman: Were Thorsen memory tubes purely a fictional creation?

Heinlein: Yes, however they've got things that are the equivalent to it right now, but I invented that notion back before they *did* have, when the state of computer art was much more primitive than it is now. I'm really surprised to see the extent to which they've managed to compress the memories in—oh, microminaturization in computers today is incredible to a person who's seen it grow up. I was first training in computers—in ballistics computers—back in 1930, when all the sequences had to be mechanical. When I see how far machine computation has gone since that time, I find it *the* most impressive development—more impressive than the atom bomb, more impressive than space travel—in its final consequences.

Schulman: How far away do you think we are before somebody like Mike will be around?

Heinlein: You mean a human being who is raised by other beings?
Schulman: No, I mean Mike in *The Moon is a Harsh*

Mistress.

Heinlein: Oh!

Schulman: Or is it the same character, as some people have claimed?

Heinlein: Uh, no. Simple coincidence. The names *derive* differently. One is from Mycroft and the other is from Michael. Combined with the fact that I have habitually used rather commonplace names for my lead characters on purpose.

Schulman: I noticed at least four characters with the name "Smith"—or "Smythe" if you include—

Heinlein: Yes. Uh, huh. That's on purpose. If you don't use commonplace names then you invest a character with something unusual by his name. Now, Dr. Jubal Harshaw is an unusual name and there's a reason for it...there are overtones to the thing. Jonathan Hoag is an unusual name, and I spent a lot of time picking out that name. But ordinarily I use very commonplace names because I want the reader to identify: this is an everyman character.

Schulman: But anyway, getting back to Mike in *The Moon is a Harsh Mistress...*

Heinlein: Now, that has an assumption in it that we

don't know to be true and the assumption is discussed still farther in *Time Enough For Love*. The assumption is that once a computer gets sufficiently complex—on the order of complexity of the human brain—that awareness can take place, self awareness. Now, that's purely an assumption—I don't know whether it's true or not—but then nobody knows how human consciousness works, either. Herman Kahn was a guest of ours at the time I was writing *The Moon is a Harsh Mistress*. Do you know who I mean? The Hudson Institute?

Schulman: Uh, no I don't.

Heinlein: *On Thermonuclear Warfare? Thinking About the Unthinkable? On Escalation?* Never heard of Herman Kahn?

Schulman: I'm afraid I'm abysmally ignorant.

Heinlein: Well, he was with the Rand corporation, then he set up his own think-tank up the Hudson called the Hudson Institute. He is widely regarded as one of the top brains in the country. He was a physicist before he became an interdisciplinary man. I told him about this assumption and Herman thought about it and said, "Yes, that appears plausible." He made no further comment, because it's a matter on which no one can have a finished opinion until we see. This matter of artificial intelligence isn't very far along, yet—even the stuff they're doing at M.I.T.

Schulman: Marvin Minsky and Seymour Pappert?

Heinlein: Yes, Marvin—you saw the article about Marvin in the *Wall Street Journal* about two weeks ago?

Schulman: No, I didn't. The whole thing was pointed out to me by J.J. Pierce. [See "An interview With John J. Pierce," NLN 21, May, 1973 for this reference.]

Heinlein: Uh, huh. Marvin doesn't make any more claim than that himself. We were shipmates here a short time ago—he and his daughter and my wife and myself—and we had a little discussion. There are some of us who think that machine intelligence is possible—machine self awareness—and some who do not, but the matter is wide open at the present time—nobody knows. Certainly Dr. Minsky has done pretty well in the line of teaching machines to do things. His machines *do* appear to reason. Remember and reason, but on a fairly primitive scale.

Let's see. This came about as the result of someone saying that you ought to do a movie star-type interview.

Schulman: We seem to get back to the weighty stuff.

Heinlein: Well, let's see. I suppose that you have the usual biographical stuff on me that's been carried in several books several times?

Schulman: I have all sorts of stuff. Alexei Panshin gives a brief account, there's a brief account in *The Past Through Tomorrow*, I have a sheet which I Xerox[-copied] from a library book [*Contemporary American Authors*]…Yeah I have several things.

Heinlein: I don't know what Panshin had to say because I've never read anything by Panshin. Panshin doesn't know very much about me, that's certain, I've never met him.

Schulman: I don't know. I really think you may have missed something by not reading *Heinlein in Dimension*; I really found it a fascinating book.

Heinlein: Look, I don't ordinarily read reviews; my publisher does—he keeps track of them. I would read such a book if it were about Isaac Asimov, but although I know Isaac very well—close friend from a long time back—in reading about Isaac I would be reading about another person. Why the devil should I read about myself—what for?

Schulman: Well, much of the material in the book is not specifically about you, it's about other concepts in science fiction and relating it to where he feels your contributions have been.

Heinlein: Well, okay. But still, why would I read it? I *wrote* it! [Laughter] I'm *certainly* not the market he aimed it at.

Schulman: No, I guess not.

Heinlein: Yes.

Schulman: One thing which I have a note on here—which doesn't relate to the movie-star interview part—is that there's a notion in several of your books—I'm specifically thinking of *Podkayne*—about Man's limitations in his own environment. You know, about how he can be sunstruck very easily, and needs arch-supports, and all sorts of things like that.

Heinlein: I didn't hear that latter part.

Schulman: That he needs arch-supports for his feet.

Heinlein: Oh, yes.

Schulman: Yes. And one of the notions that came to mind when you related to this how you thought that perhaps this wasn't man's natural environment was Desmond Morris's theory that the missing link in Man's evolution was a stage as an *aquatic* animal. I was wondering what you thought about that?

Heinlein: Well, it doesn't seem very likely to me, but it's not a matter to which I've given any deep thought. I haven't read what he has to say; it seems to me unlikely but I haven't read it. That's simply a very horseback opinion. It reminded me of something else...Have you read a book called *The Naked Ape*?

Schulman: Yes, that's the one I was referring to. That's by Morris.

Heinlein: Oh! And that's the book you were referring to?

Schulman: Yes. Desmond Morris's *The Naked Ape* and also *The Human Zoo*.

Heinlein: I had forgotten that portion in there about the possibility that he was aquatic—the Missing Link. The thing that impressed me about that book was his emphasis on pair-linking as an evolutionary necessity for the human animal. I was thinking about this matter...that all this discussion of sex and so forth is not appropriate to science fiction? Well, to my mind, sex is so central an element in every human being and in the development of the human race that to have left it out of science fiction—as it was for many years—was a major fault in science fiction, and I'm very pleased that it's now possible to write about it. I'm reminded of an elderly maiden aunt of a person of my generation— this was quite a while back—who remarked with re- spect to *Romeo and Juliet* that it was an excellent play, but why did he have to get all that sex stuff into it? Human sexuality is so major a factor in the human race that any attempt to deal with the human race or with people realistically which *omits* this factor cannot really be a mature treatment. And yet I know there are people who would be made uneasy in some fashion if sex gets into it, and yet sex has to be in it if we're to have human beings...

Schulman: I'm getting near the end of the third side of my cassette; we've been going at it now for about three hours and your voice must be getting pretty tired.

Heinlein: Has it been that long? I suppose so. Let's see. As to other parts about me personally, you have some biog-notes there. You no doubt know that I was born in Missouri, I'm sure you know that I went to the Naval Academy and that I was disabled out of the Navy. I'm one of a large family. I have two older brothers—one of them is a general and one a professor—and one younger brother who is a professor, and three sisters. It's a very long-lived family. My mother is still living at ninety-four...And [my grandfather taught] me to play chess when I was four years old and we used to play.

Schulman: Do you still play?

Heinlein: I haven't time. I haven't time. Chess and contract bridge are both very entertaining and they are both compelling time-takers. I've given up both of them because they take up so much time. And, essentially there's nothing to either one of them—I mean after you're through where have you been? Like the boy who rode the merry-go-round. I just haven't time; there's too much to do. No, I expect to take up both of them again when I *do* finally retire—if I ever do.

Schulman: I didn't know that writers *did* retire.

Heinlein: Well, Tony Boucher pointed that out to me years ago. He said that there are retired everything else—retired schoolteachers, retired firemen, retired bankers—but there are no retired writers. There are simply writers who are no longer selling.

Schulman: I assume that you say, "Dammit, I'm going to retire" and then two hours later you say, "Hey—I just got the greatest idea for a story!"

Heinlein: Oh, yes. It's addictive. I didn't intend to stay in the writing business more than a couple of years.

Schulman: There's a statement made to that effect in your forty-one Worldcon speech; you said that you'd probably be doing something along the line of defense work.

Heinlein: Well, yes...
[Break in transcription as cassette ended. Question asked before I realized it wasn't going dealt with whether he thought events of today were indicative of a "future shock" similar to the "semantic disorientation" of the Crazy Years in the "Future History" series—JNS]

Schulman: Okay. I think we're going again.

Heinlein: [Responding in the affirmative] A very easy example is right there in Manhattan. Back in 1930 I had a studio down in Greenwich Village and I never hesitated to be out at night any place in Manhattan. Now when I go to Manhattan I am very, very careful. The situation has changed. Even though that was during Prohibition—the so-called gangster era—the streets were far safer then than they are now. Mugging didn't even exist as a word in 1930. That's one illustration.

Schulman: And certainly the word "gay" has changed in meaning considerably.

Heinlein: Well, it has changed in the public meaning. "Gay" had its idiomatic meaning in respect to homosexuality—"among the gay"—as far back as 1930. I know, for of course Greenwich Village even then had quite a lot of it, both men and women. But "gay"—now the general public knows what it means. I mean the idiomatic meaning has pushed the normal meaning aside. If you read over the headlines that I put into the *Crazy Years* in *Methuselah's Children*, some of them don't even look odd.

Schulman: No, they don't.

Heinlein: They're not startling. But they *were* startling when I wrote them.

Schulman: Although nobody's talking about raising the voting age to forty-one.

Heinlein: No, but they did the reverse of that; they lowered it to eighteen, and they removed all possible impediments. I mean, all you have to be is a warm body now. For example at the present time, the student body down here at the University of California at Santa Cruz is eligible to vote in the city election—any of them who care to register for it—by the current rulings. This means the student body can outvote the city itself on things like bond elections. On the real property. And yet those kids down there are transients. They're not permanent residents, they're simply there to go to school.

Schulman: I never *did* think voting was a very good way to settle issues.

Heinlein: I don't either, and neither does Lazarus Long, as I indicated in there. But the things that they've done about voting are the reverse of what I had in there about raising the voting age to forty. It would have fitted more if I had made it "lowered the voting age to twelve."

Schulman: Well there was a movie about that just a short time ago.
Heinlein: Yes, I know. I didn't see the movie but I read

an account of it. I know that there was such.

Schulman: *Wild in the Streets.*

Heinlein: Yes, *Wild in the Streets*, and they were liquidating people who were over something or other.

Schulman: I think it was thirty.

Heinlein: Something like that.

Schulman: Taking them off to prison camps.

Heinlein: Yes. I remember the *Wall Street Journal* ran a three line notice—sad note or obituary, or something like that; this was four or five years ago—noting that the man who originated the slogan, "Never trust anyone over thirty"?

Schulman: Yes?

Heinlein: Had just had his thirtieth birthday. [Laughter] This was four or five years back.

Schulman: Tell me, what do you mean by a "mature society"? You used the words differently on the "Future History" chart and in *Time Enough For Love*. Like on the "Future History" chart you refer to the semantically oriented society as a "mature" society. End of human adolescence.

Heinlein: And in *Time Enough For Love*?

Schulman: There's a sentence to the effect that in a "mature society" civil servant is semantically equivalent to civil *master*.

Heinlein: Yes. Well, you can attribute that to the fact that in the course of thirty years, I became some what pessimistic about political solutions. Yes, I did use the word differently. At the time I wrote *Methuselah's Children* I was still politically quite naive and still had hopes that various libertarian notions could be put over by political processes....It [now] seems to me that every time we manage to establish one freedom, they take another one away. Maybe two. And that seems to me characteristic of a society as it gets older and more crowded and higher taxes and more laws. One thing that I stuck in *Time enough For Love* on purpose without calling attention to it had this twelve-year-old boy driving a car in Kansas City? And Lazarus thought it was all right and legal at that time in Kansas City. My next older brother drove a car regularly—every day—when he was twelve years old in Kansas City. There were neither driving examinations nor driving licenses. Nor very much traffic.

Schulman: I don't know. I'm sort of hoping that one of these days we'll get the best of both worlds, the high technology that we benefit so much by—which we need a fairly large population for—and the libertarian society which I'm working for.

Heinlein: The question of how many mega-men it takes to maintain a high-technology society and how many mega-men it takes to produce oppressions simply through the complexity of the society is a matter that I have never satisfactorily solved in my own mind. but I am quite sure that one works against the other, that it takes a large-ish population for a high technology, but if you get large populations human liberties are *automatically* restricted even if you don't have legislation about it. In fact, the legislation in many cases is intended to—and sometimes does—lubricate the frictions that take place between people simply because they're too close together.

Schulman: I'm sort of thinking the solution might come *through* technology, if we ever get to the point where you have some sort of, let's say, portable force-field which can physically prevent a person from being harmed by somebody else.

Heinlein: Have you read *The Caves of Steel* and *The Naked Sun* by Dr. Asimov?

Schulman: No, I haven't.

Heinlein: I think they're in hardcover and in the library. One shows a highly libertarian society and the other one shows Manhattan even more crowded that it is now. And Isaac deals with each of them—somewhat different in point of view from you or from me—because Isaac actually *likes* big cities.

Schulman: Well, so do I. One of my favorite lines in all your writings is the description of New Chicago in *Between Planets* with its decadence—"rotten at the core and skidding toward the pit"—that's just the type of place I like. I guess I—like Dr. Jefferson—"infest" New York.

Heinlein: You would find both those Asimov books interesting particularly if you read them practically side by side. There's the same historical background and one concerns an extremely *loose* population and the other one concerns and extremely *tight* population and how they deal with it. Isaac's stuff is *always* stimulating even when you don't agree with it. Perhaps even most so when you disagree with it.

Well, unless you have something else specifically to ask me, I think we'd better simply adjourn.

Schulman: Well, I just have one more question…Do you expect a "false dawn" and eclipse in astronautics?

Heinlein: Oh, hell. [Laughter] That *whole* chart is fictional. The stuff isn't history, it's *fiction.* Anybody who would attempt to make a firm prediction about that with the amount of data at hand would be reckless, to say the least. There doesn't seem to be any great enthusiasm for space travel at the present time in this country but I'm reasonably certain that the human race will continue with it in the near future. Whether or not they'll do it in English, or in Russian, or in Chinese, I couldn't guess. But I don't think we've dropped the matter.

Schulman: If you really ever get interested in the Prophet again, I'm still waiting to find out about him. He interests me.

Heinlein: What—Nehemiah Scudder?

Schulman: Yes.

Heinlein: Oh, I might some day. I don't know.

Schulman: He's the one character you've created that we've never met, yet.

Heinlein: That was intentional. One of the things I had in mind was to do a story in which the lead character would never come on stage. What you would feel is his influence. And I think I did.

Schulman: Well, I guess I've sort of talked myself out. At least for now...[Deletion of some technical conversation]
Heinlein: Well, I'll talk further if you want to at another

time.

Schulman: Thank you very, very much Mr. Heinlein.

Heinlein: I look forward to hearing from you again. Goodbye.

Schulman: Bye, bye.

Letter to Brad Linaweaver

14 July 1987

Dear Brad,

Re. your post card on *To Sail Beyond the Sunset.* I guess I'm not inclined to review it publicly, as I did with *Job*, because I have the awful feeling—from the ending—that this might be Heinlein signing off fiction writing, and I don't want to contend with this. I will say, privately, that I think this novel demonstrates that Heinlein has successfully showed his critics that he can, indeed, write female characters with the best of them.

As for the swipes at revisionism contained therein, I noticed them too, but I would like to note the following.

As you recall, Bob Wilson wrote an article in *NL* chiding me for a sign in *Alongside Night* that read, "No Dogs or Welfare Parasites," and used my inclusion of this sign in my novel as evidence that the author hated the poor. Neal Wilgus brought this up again in my *SFR* interview. And what I said in both cases is that one should not hold an author responsible for opinions expressed by a fictional character in that author's novels. You might also recall that in my author's note beginning *Rainbow Cadenza*, I explicitly state, "The opinions ... of the characters in this book should not be taken as being the author's own or those of any real person. If there's anything I want to pin myself down on, I'll do it in my own voice." I certainly pinned myself down in the glossary on a number of points "in my own voice" and, since *Rainbow* was written third person, my own voice was heard in some places in the novel's exposition as well.

I'm extending to Mr. Heinlein the courtesy I asked Wilson and Wilgus to extend me. *To Sail Beyond the Sunset* is written first person in the voice of Maureen; Heinlein's *own* voice is never heard. Maureen is *characterized* as expressing anti-revisionist viewpoints by her first-person statements. This is therefore as much *the author's statement about that character* as it is a statement of that character's view on a particular issue. Maureen is on record regarding revisionism; to the best of my recollection, Heinlein is not.

If we want to know Mr. Heinlein's viewpoint on revisionism, we'll still have to ask him.

[Some personal material deleted.]

All best,

Neil

The Moon Is A Harsh Mistress
Reviewed by J. Neil Schulman

Many libertarians practice a religious dogma which I'll term "Monovelism." The Sacred Creed of the Monovelist is "There is But One True Novel, It's Name Is *Atlas Shrugged*, and I Will Have No Other Novels Before *It*."

Or after it, judging by the depressing sales figures Laissez Faire Books has had on novels by myself, Victor Koman, L. Neil Smith, and Brad Linaweaver, as compared to Laissez Faire's sales on *Atlas Shrugged*—or compared to its sales figures on its more popular nonfiction books, for that matter.

Let me be blunt about this. If you think Ayn Rand's novels are the last word on libertarian fiction, then you are as bigoted in your thinking as any TV evangelist who preaches that the *only* stories we need to read are in the King James Bible.

For me, libertarianism didn't start with Ayn Rand. In fact, *Atlas Shrugged* was recommended to me when I was 14. I lifted it off the library shelf, saw how many pages were in the damn thing, and put it right back. I didn't pick up a copy again for another four years, and by that time I had already started a libertarian group on my college campus.

The author who made me a libertarian wasn't Ayn Rand but Robert A. Heinlein.

Of his 45 or so books, the novel which was most influential in getting me to start thinking like a libertarian, and *instantly* to recognize libertarians as ideological kin when I first encountered them, was *The Moon Is A Harsh Mistress.*

The Moon Is A Harsh Mistress tells the story of a revolutionary war fought against the one-world government of Earth by colonists on *Luna*, Earth's moon, in the year 2076. It's no coincidence that Heinlein set his parable precisely three centuries after the American Revolution because much of Heinlein's future parallels our nation's past: a repressive absentee government set on economic exploitation of a new world for its own benefit and *only* its own benefit.

The story of the revolution is told first person by Manuel Garcia O'Kelly, a computer tech working for the Lunar Authority. In a 1973 interview I did with Heinlein, he confessed how surprised he was by the speed of computer progress; *Moon* reflects this in a future without an Internet of personal computers, but instead a central mainframe with as many connections as the neural network of the human brain. Heinlein had asked scientist Herman Kahn whether a computer with equivalent connections might think; Kahn had answered, "That seems plausible." Kahn's plausibility became the nexus of Heinlein's novel. The computer, a "HOLMES Mark IV" computer which Manuel O'Kelly names Mycroft after Sherlock's brother and addresses as "Mike" (the computer returns the favor by nicknaming Manuel "Man")—is much smarter than HAL in *2001*—smart enough to become the eyes, ears, Internet server, and brain of a revolution.

The plot takes shape when O'Kelly—in consultations with friends including Mike, a Benjamin Franklin-type revolututionary named Professor Bernardo de la Paz, and a rabble-rousing feminist named Wyoming Knott—learns that the lunar colony is just a few years from planetary starvation caused by the Earth authority's economic policies. There is no institutional means of staving off impending doom which leaves revolution as the only chance for colonial survival.

Heinlein uses the causes and situations of this future society as blueprints for political and sociological change. In Heinlein's future *Luna*, a fully privatized social system has been developed, one where custom and market institutions have entirely replaced government.

Any marriage contract—polyandry, group marriages, whatever—is socially accepted. Private arbitration has replaced courts, and decisions including the death penalty are enforced by popular acclaim. Education, insurance, and banking are entirely private matters. Heinlein's anarchic legal system is so well worked out that the *Tennessee Law Review* examined it seriously, in a Fall, 1995 article by Dmitry Feofanov titled "Luna Law: The Libertarian Vision in Heinlein's *The Moon Is A Harsh Mistress*."

Here you'll learn that the essence of "rational anarchism" is the understanding that personal responsibility for one's actions are neither increased nor lessened by hiding an action behind the curtain of governmental sovereignty.

You'll discover the principle of TANSTAAFL—"There Ain't *N*o *S*uch *T*hing *A*s *A F*ree *L*unch"—which demolishes all socialist schemes which try to increase the public good by redistributing wealth.

The Moon Is A Harsh Mistress mines as rich a vein of ideas on both political and social concerns as *Atlas Shrugged.* If you decide to break free from the chains of Monovelism, there's no better place to start.

Prometheus Hall of Fame Acceptance Speech for *Methuselah's Children,*
LoneStarCon, San Antonio, Texas, 1997

The Hall of Fame award was set up by the Libertarian Futurist Society to honor works of fiction which were published before there was a Prometheus Award. Or at least, old enough that they can now qualify for the Hall of Fame award. The works have to be published ten years before being eligible for the Award.

This year's finalists for the Hall of Fame are *Emphyrio* by Jack Vance, *Oath of Fealty* by Larry Niven and Jerry Pournelle, *Little Fuzzy* by H. Beam Piper, *A Planet for Texans* by H. Beam Piper, and *Methuselah's Children* by Robert A. Heinlein.

Now, I'm here both to present the award, and accept the award, on behalf of the winner, *Methuselah's Children* by Robert A. Heinlein.

In preparation for accepting the award, I've been rereading the book. This is a novel I haven't read probably for ten years, although I've read it a number of times.

It was originally published in *Astounding* in 1941, written in 1940, I assume. I think it establishes Heinlein as a prophet. He has the ability to understand the future, more so than almost anyone else I can think of. His accuracy is astonishing. I think the best example of that, is that Heinlein describes, from his vantage point in 1941, headlines from April through June, 1969. I'd like to read to you some of the selected headlines from April through June, 1969, which Heinlein described as "that period during the World Wars, sometimes loosely termed 'the crazy years.'"

Baby Bill Breaks Bank
2-Year Toddler Youngest Winner $1 Mil TV Jackpot
White House Phones Congrats

I think Heinlein understood the dynamics of the Clinton administration very well.

Court Orders Statehouse Sold
Colorado Supreme Bench Rules State Old Age
Pension Has First Lien All State Property

I think Heinlein well understood the economics of the Clinton administration.

New York Youth Meet Demands Upper Limit On Franchise

U.S. Birth Rate 'Top Secret'—Defense Sec

Carolina Congressman Cops Beauty Crown
"Available for draft for president" she announces while starting tour to show her qualifications

Heinlein definitely had an understanding of the politics of our age.

Earth-Eating Fad Moves West:
Chicago Parson East Clay Sandwich in Pulpit

And now we get to a couple of these headlines that I commented on when I interviewed Heinlein back in the early 1970s. These didn't even sound odd at the time, or now.

Los Angeles High School Mob Defies School Board
Higher Pay, Shorter Hours, No Schoolwork—
We Demand Our Right To Elect Teachers

By the time 1969 came around, that's exactly what they were doing. And again, one that doesn't seem at all odd now:

Suicide Rate Up Ninth Successive Year

But, predictions about 1969 were perhaps the least of what Heinlein was doing in this 1941 novel. Heinlein, in essence, predicted the Holocaust.

You have here a group of people, the Howard Families, who are very much like latter-day Jews. Basically, the Howard Families have separated themselves from the rest of humanity through breeding—in this case, breeding for long life. You have a group of people who are regularly living into their 150's, and 160's, and 170's.

The first thing that happens when they reveal their longevity is that everybody wants to round them up and get this secret to long life out of them, even if they have to kill them along the way. [Like many other Heinlein ideas, this one has been picked up by other writers—most recently by the screenwriters of *Star Trek: Insurrection.*—JNS, 1999]

So you have a group here which is singled out by a society that supposedly believes in rights and civil liberties. But the minute anything inconvenient comes along they immediately throw the rights and civil liberties out the window.

What you have here is a textbook description by Heinlein, of how guarantees on paper don't mean anything if people decide that there is something they want.

Heinlein, introducing the character for the first time of Lazarus Long, has Lazarus hiding all his weapons from a society which doesn't believe in carrying personal weapons.

Lazarus comments to himself that there are no dangerous weapons, only dangerous people. That's typical of the gems of wisdom that are sprinkled throughout the book.

If Victor Koman's *Kings of the High Frontier* [receiving the Prometheus Award at the same ceremony—JNS] was about the engineering of private space flight, Lazarus Long had a simpler solution: simply steal a space ship! [Laughter] Hey, nobody was in it so go ahead and grab it.

But, *Methuselah's Children* is just a wonderful book and just a wonderful description of the ideal of what libertarianism could create, and how fragile it is.

Heinlein discussed concepts here—many of which

he got in reading on General Semantics—which had to do with social dynamics: how people can be whipped up into a frenzy very quickly.

Heinlein understood the dynamics of mass hysteria, the jealousy against any sort of extreme wealth. For that reason alone this book would be worthy of a Prometheus Hall of Fame Award.

Overall, Heinlein, in his writing career, examined not just one scenario, but dozens of different scenarios, describing how precious human liberty is, and how difficult it is to achieve it.

On behalf of that, I'm delighted once again to be able to accept the Prometheus Hall of Fame Award for Robert Heinlein.

Requiem

1988

I reread his books and discover lines of dialogue that I unconsciously plagiarized, then think that he would've said not to worry about such thefts—"Just file off the serial numbers, run it across the state line and it's yours."

When Jascha Heifetz, considered by many of his colleagues to be the finest concert violinist of all time, died late last year, fellow virtuoso Isaac Stern said, "Heifetz has been in the inner ear of every violinist of our time."

So, too, with Heinlein and science fiction writers: he is inside our heads, and we often decide whether or not something works by the way he did it.

The buzzing in our heads doesn't stop when we leave our writing desks.

I couldn't help thinking about Heinlein last week, with a smile of recognition, when Donald Regan's book broke the news that the First Lady has been guiding presidential affairs with the help of an astrologer. I thought: So? Heinlein told us this could happen almost thirty years ago in *Stranger in a Strange Land*. One could only hope, for the sake of avoiding World War III, that Nancy Reagan's astrologer had the common sense of Heinlein's fictional Becky Vesey.

I halfway think that it couldn't have been something as silly as emphysema that killed him—it must've been the thought that his Commander-in-Chief took this sort of nonsense seriously.

Then, there's still a part of me, which has never grown any older than eight, that is halfway convinced that it's got to be a put-up job. Heinlein die? Impossible. Nothing could kill that old rascal. He's just stepped through a portal into the Rejuvenation Clinic on Tellus Tertius; when he comes back (if he finds this backwater planet worth visiting again) he'll have a biological age of eighteen and a cosmetic age of about fifty. (Old enough to keep him out of stupid bar fights.) Obviously the remains that the Navy's going to give burial-at-sea were a never-alive clone, aged for the purpose of pulling off this masquerade.

It's got to be true, doesn't it? After all, Robert A. Heinlein told the House Select Committee on Aging that he refused to die until he could die on the moon, and he wouldn't perjure himself to the United States Congress, would he?

END

About the Author

J. Neil Schulman is the author of two Prometheus award-winning novels, *Alongside Night* and *The Rainbow Cadenza*, and seven other books. He has written short fiction, nonfiction, and screenwritings, including the CBS *Twilight Zone* episode "Profile in Silver." Mr. Schulman is Chairman and Publisher of Pulpless.Com, Inc.